"I'm bullish on Tim Muehlhoff. He's authentic. He's anchored in truth. He's passionate about helping and equipping people. And he is a brilliant communicator. He doesn't just grab your attention, his pithy writing will transform your life and marriage. Buy this book. Read and apply it. In the months that follow, the climate in your marriage will improve!"

DR. DENNIS RAINEY, president, FamilyLife, and host, *FamilyLife Today*

"Effective communication—speaking the truth in love to one another—is an essential skill for a strong, healthy marriage. Dr. Muehlhoff understands much more than principles for effective communication. He understands how the gospel fundamentally reorders our relationships and changes how we relate to each other. That's what makes this book so helpful for couples who are committed to a God-glorifying marriage."

BOB LEPINE, cohost, *FamilyLife Today*

"Every time Tim Muehlhoff gets up to speak, he commands the audience's attention from start to finish. I am among his biggest fans, adjusting my schedule to hear his always creative, poignant, funny and God-honoring words. His gift of communication in an auditorium is not outdone by his gift of communication in a book. In his new book, *Marriage Forecasting,* Tim is refreshingly transparent and honest as he lays out an antidote to the miscommunications that get in the way of so many of us married types. What makes this book even more important to me is that I know Tim, a regular guy who wrestles like the rest of us with how to make a marriage work well and long. Once again through these pages, I marvel at Tim's remarkable ability to communicate biblical truth in real-world ways."

BARRY H. COREY, Ph.D., president, Biola University

"Every marriage has a climate, and we don't know a better weather forecaster than Tim Muehlhoff. In every relationship there are either fair skies or storm clouds gathering overhead; Tim will show you how to end the rain and bring back the sunny skies you've been missing. Tim is a masterful communicator who makes his points with humor and compassion—this is an excellent book."

TIM AND JOY DOWNS, authors of *Fight Fair* and *One of Us Must Be Crazy*

"Dr. Tim Muehlhoff has written a thought-provoking book that is a masterful blend of insight, humor and experience. It is rich with up-to-date, relevant and hopeful advice concerning relationships and marriage. If your desire is to make your friendships better, to navigate (and even thrive!) during the inevitable storms of marriage, or simply to reference a trusted source on communication and conflict, this is your book. It is practical, compelling and a thoroughly enjoyable read that shows you how to improve and strengthen your marriage climate."

CHRISTOPHER GRACE, Ph.D., vice president and professor of psychology, Biola University

Marriage Forecasting

Changing the Climate of Your Relationship
One Conversation at a Time

TIM MUEHLHOFF

FOREWORD BY DAN B. ALLENDER

IVP Books
An imprint of InterVarsity Press
Downers Grove, Illinois

InterVarsity Press
P.O. Box 1400, Downers Grove, IL 60515-1426
World Wide Web: www.ivpress.com
E-mail: email@ivpress.com

InterVarsity Press® is the book-publishing division of InterVarsity Christian Fellowship/USA®, a
movement of students and faculty active on campus at hundreds of universities, colleges and schools
of nursing in the United States of America, and a member movement of the International Fellowship
of Evangelical Students. For information about local and regional activities, write Public Relations
Dept., InterVarsity Christian Fellowship/USA, 6400 Schroeder Rd., P.O. Box 7895, Madison, WI
53707-7895, or visit the IVCF website at <www.intervarsity.org>.

All Scripture quotations, unless otherwise indicated, are taken from the Holy Bible, New
International Version®. NIV®. Copyright ©1973, 1978, 1984 by International Bible Society. Used
by permission of Zondervan Publishing House. All rights reserved.

While all stories in this book are true, some names and identifying information in this book have
been changed to protect the privacy of the individuals involved.

Design: Cindy Kiple
Images: Dave & Les Jacobs/Getty Images

ISBN 978-0-8308-3841-7

Printed in Canada

Library of Congress Cataloging-in-Publication Data

Muehlhoff, Tim, 1961-
    Marriage forecasting: changing the climate of your relationship one
conversation at a time / Tim Muehlhoff.
        p. cm.
    Includes bibliographical references (p.).
    ISBN 978-0-8308-3841-7 (pbk.: alk. paper)
    1. Marriage—Religious aspects—Christianity. 2.
Communication—Religious aspects—Christianity. I. Title.
BV825.M78   2010
248.8'44—dc22

                                                            2010024968

P	18	17	16	15	14	13	12	11	10	9	8	7	6	5	4	3	2	1
Y	25	24	23	22	21	20	19	18	17	16	15	14	13	12	11	10

For Noreen,

who fills my climate with

love and encouragement,

and to Jeremy, Michael and Jason,

who fill it with laughter!

Contents

Foreword

The rain ripped across the soccer field in dervish frenzy. It was early June and our second week living in Seattle. I stood talking to a fellow parent about whether this was what we needed to expect all summer. He smiled. "You must be new to the area. No, this rain is quite uncommon, but can I offer you some sage advice we were given when we first moved here?" His demeanor was attentive and kind. Like any immigrant to a new land I was desperate for local knowledge, and I eagerly indicated I wanted his counsel.

He told me that his first year in Seattle had been miserable. They planned a cookout and it rained, and they canceled. They were going for a run, it rained and they stayed indoors. The weather began to ruin their lives. He suffered a bout of Seasonal Affective Disorder Syndrome and, after a dreary wet winter, wanted to move. And then a neighbor gave him a Norwegian proverb in a time of major despair. He was told, "There is no bad weather, only bad clothing."

He waited for my response after offering this tidbit of wisdom. I wanted to laugh, cry, scream, but instead I said, "Well, that should make REI happy." We passed from that conversa-

tion to the banalities of being soccer dads and I never saw him
again after the game.

His words haunt me from over twelve years ago. They have
proven prophetically true and are a profound gift. First, we all
must take the weather seriously every day of our lives. Tragically we know how to read the weather but seldom read the
larger context of how we are living our lives and the atmosphere
in the room or in our relationships.

I am fascinated by weather. It has actually become a realm of
study, intrigue and daily fascination. I don't just check out the
weather report, I click on the NASA website where I can see the
weather patterns developing in the Pacific to see what I can
expect over the next week. It is the play of prediction, planning
and submission to mystery, and the full acknowledgment that
as much as I know, there is more that I don't know. I spend time
thinking about the weather every day.

Yet I don't spend nearly the same amount of time studying
the atmosphere of my relationship with my wife. A word can
turn our world to clammy and suffocating humidity. A sentence
can turn a bright day into the shadows of a brewing thunder-
storm. It is a metaphor; it is a reality. It is crucial to read the
weather. This brilliant book will give you the language we use
daily in one realm to use in a domain we seldom name or consider. You'll find in a brief period of time you are seeing and
experiencing things that make vastly more sense because you
have language that tells the truth and gives you new capacity to
make change.

The proverb I learned from my soccer acquaintance uses
hyperbole—is there no bad weather? Of course, we know there
is good and bad weather. Yet like any proverb it also tells the
truth—when you have good clothing, foul weather is no longer
a danger and perhaps at times even a pleasure. I have at times,
since the purchase of "good clothing," sat outdoors in the mid-

dle of a rainstorm for hours, allowing the cold, incessant sheets of rain to pour down on me and wash me of my thoughts and burdens. It has been healing to encounter extremity with the provision of good clothes.

Tim not only offers a useful language to name the seasons and movements of our marriages, he also gives us the blessing of new clothes. He dresses us for the searing heat, the cacophony of thunder and lightning, and the cold, hollow recesses of winter. He offers us the pleasure of knowing the weather and being prepared to enter not merely to survive but to thrive in the face of all that the world around us can do. I love this book. I know Tim and Noreen, and my respect for their love and passion for Jesus and each other and their children and ministries is vast. He is a man I'd listen to if he talked about Charlie Brown or the mysteries of ontology.

I suspect what you will find as you read this book is a profound relief and hope that someone has finally said what we all have felt in our marriages but for some reason didn't say before. And far more, I know your heart will venture farther and more richly into realms of hope that you too can say there is no bad weather in my marriage, only the provision of God, his good clothing, to cover us from shame and fear. May the wind of God be at your back, the delight of God be as the warm glow of the sun, and may you read this glorious book with anticipation and joy.

Dan B. Allender, Ph.D.
Professor and Founding President,
Mars Hill Graduate School

Acknowledgments

I would like to thank Jon Lunde, Chris Grace, Stacy Mushakian and Lynda Bryant for allowing me to share early ideas and drafts of this book with them. Rachel Beck, thanks for tracking down obscure articles and sources! A special thanks goes to my friend V. J. Vonk, who read *every* word of early drafts and not only offered keen editorial input but, more importantly, timely encouragement. Miss you around the department! To Dennis Rainey, thank you for allowing me to have a platform to develop and refine my ideas about marriage. I'm indebted to Al Hsu for his patience, thorough suggestions and guidance on this project—I couldn't ask for a better editor. As always, *thank you* to my wife who has, for over twenty years, created a climate of commitment, trust and encouragement that allows me to follow God's calling and to shine in my gifts. Noreen, without you, my ministry—let alone this book—wouldn't be possible.

Introduction

You and your spouse sit down to have a talk. Both of you are dreading what may follow. It's the finances again. Each of you has different ideas when it comes to saving and spending, and every time the credit card bill comes, attitudes start to sour. You warn yourself not to get defensive, but as soon as the conversation starts, you are angry. "This is *my* fault?" you blurt out. Voices rise, the temperature in the room chills, and a storm starts to roll in.

Consider another storm.

In the movie *The Perfect Storm*, George Clooney's character, Billy, and his crew make the gutsy decision to sail through the North Atlantic to search for swordfish. They strike it rich. The belly of the *Andrea Gail* is filled to capacity. This catch alone will earn them more money than they made in the previous two seasons. Debts can be paid and families compensated for time spent away.

There's only one problem—the weather. The crew receives reports from shore that three massive storms, including a hurricane, are coming together to form a one-of-a-kind nor'easter. Wanting to cash in on their one-of-a-kind catch, Billy disregards the reports and pushes through the storm. They encounter the perfect storm: waves ten stories high and winds exceeding 120 miles per hour.

What do finances and Atlantic storms have to do with each other? The *Andrea Gail* faced a climate filled with driving rain, hurricane winds and ten-story waves. That's what you and your spouse face too. Attempts to discuss money put you and your spouse in the middle of a turbulent climate. You faced a *communication climate* filled with anger, discouragement and waves of defensiveness pounding in on the health of your marriage. And, like the owner of the *Andrea Gail*, you decided not to wait it out. Desiring to resolve your conflict, you tried to push through the anger and defensiveness. It didn't work.

My wife, Noreen, and I repeat the same mistakes. When faced with an issue that *must* be resolved—finances, conflicting schedules, differing priorities—we grit our teeth and force ourselves to discuss it *again*. Like the crew of the *Andrea Gail*, we batten down the hatches, stow the sails and try to push through the storm. We mistakenly think that what's needed is more communication. "Solving marital problems can be like freeing oneself from quicksand," writes one author. "The harder you try to make things better, the less things change."[1] Ironically, what may be needed is not more communication but an assessment of the environment in which communication happens.

Marriage Forecasting is based on the simple idea that marriages are a lot like the weather. Some marriages have a stable climate, while others have an unpredictable one. For some of you, the climate of your marriage is like that in Southern California—bright sunshine and wonderful predictability. For others, marriage is a lot like living in the Midwest, where they say, "If you don't like the weather, wait a five minutes and it'll change." More than likely, you are somewhere in between: seasons of turbulence, seasons of calm.

Ignoring the climate of our marriage carries severe consequences. It greatly reduces the effectiveness of our communication with each other. Couples ought to place a "Weather Permitting" sign over every conversation before it begins. Just as a runner checks the heat index and plans his or her run accordingly, marriage partners should attempt to discuss potentially volatile issues only when the climate in the marriage is conducive to positive communication. Sometimes the wisest thing a couple can do in a marriage is postpone talking about key issues and instead work on improving the general climate within the marriage.

Marriage Forecasting equips you to make a climate reading of your marriage and to develop communication strategies to improve it. The good news: communication climates are not *exactly* like the weather. While the weather outside is out of our control, the communication climate within our home is largely our responsibility.

If your current marital climate is cold and lacks intimacy, it can be improved by using some simple communication strategies. *Marriage Forecasting* applies research in the area of marital communication, listening skills, empathy and conflict resolution. While teaching on marriage for over twenty years and navigating the storms of my own marriage, I've collected some valuable strategies on adjusting the climate of a marriage.

The communication principles in this book are rooted in the wisdom of the Scriptures. You may be surprised how much the Bible has to say about conflict, forgiveness, empathy, marriage, sexual intimacy, balancing schedules, priorities and the power of words. While they do not refer to communication climates directly, the Scriptures describe the enormous influence timing and setting play in our communication. The book of Proverbs states that a word spoken in the *right circumstances* at the *right time* is "like apples of gold in settings of silver" (25:11). The conditions in which you choose to speak, suggest these wise conversationalists, are just as important as what you say.

HOW THIS BOOK IS ORGANIZED

"Don't knock the weather; nine-tenths of the people couldn't start a conversation if it didn't change once in a while," quips humorist Ken Hubbard. In this book we won't just talk about marital climates. We'll focus on how to change the climate of your marriage by considering three vital skills. First, we'll look at the four key components that make up every communication climate: acknowledgment, expectations, commitment and trust. Second, you'll learn how to take an accurate climate reading of your marriage. (Is the atmosphere of my marriage supportive or defensive? Do I feel valued? When we discuss sensitive issues, what do I expect to happen—debate or dialogue?) Third, you'll come to understand how to steadily improve the relational climate of your marriage. Chapter four introduces you to the key idea of relational investments that can over time strengthen a couple's sense of commitment.

Specifically, this book will help you do the following:

- Recognize how the cultural climate surrounding you influences your marital climate.
- Identify words and actions that foster a positive communication climate.
- Invest thirty seconds a day to keep a positive climate strong.
- Understand what causes a poor communication climate to develop.
- Stop negative communication from spiraling out of control.
- Effectively assess conflict.
- Understand the role gender plays in creating positive or negative climates.

- Rebuild trust in your relationship if trust has been severed.

- Call a truce in your marriage.

- Understand how your relationship with God deeply influences your marriage.

Mountain climbers have a saying: "You can't schedule a summit. You can only hope for one." The climate surrounding a mountain will dictate what you can or can't do on any given day. In the history of Mt. Everest, more than 120 climbers have died trying to climb it. Many of these experienced climbers perished because they, like the crew of the *Andrea Gail*, worked against the climate, not with it. Success was within the grasp of each of these climbers. All they needed to do was be patient and wait for bad weather to break. The good news about communication climates is that we don't have to helplessly wait for them to improve. We can make the change happen.

What Are Communication Climates?

*W*hile at a dinner party, we sat with some friends who are ardent campers. They told story after story of pitching tents next to streams, going to sleep in thermal underwear and waking at sunrise to catch breakfast. Noreen and I chuckled as we listened. Shifting the conversation to us, they asked if we liked to camp. Noreen laughed and said, "No. Tim's not that hardy."

I also laughed, but became increasingly silent and defensive. I could feel a strong chill blow through our climate. I interpreted the word *hardy* to be a dig at my masculinity. For the rest of the dinner party, I was cool and distant toward Noreen.

During the ride home, Noreen could feel the shift in our climate and asked what was wrong. After I repeated her comment, she was immediately apologetic and explained that she simply meant I am not the outdoorsy type. She's right. Growing up, my two older brothers and I were so involved in sports that there was no time to go camping. As a result, my idea of roughing it is to stay at a hotel that doesn't have ESPN in HD.

Have there been times your spouse has said something that

hurt you or made you angry, and it shut down communication? Once the communication climate between you and your spouse is disrupted, it's difficult and even unwise to ignore. And ignoring a communication climate is as futile as ignoring the climate outside your door.

I know, I've tried. My friend and I—both tennis junkies— once got a case of cabin fever in the middle of January in Michigan. On the first sunny day, with the temperature just above freezing, we grabbed our rackets and snow shovels, and headed off to some outdoor courts. Except for looking extremely odd, our plan seemed to work—for a while. During one rally, a partially frozen ball slammed *through* the frigid strings of my racket. Game over.

That day we learned a painful lesson: Mother Nature will not be ignored. The climate outside your door determines when and what activities you can do, from tennis to picnics to a trip to the beach. The same is true of the communication climate that surrounds our marriages. It's possible to ignore a wintery marital climate for a while, but it will eventually compromise your ability to communicate with each other. A key step to improving communication with your spouse is to understand the overall climate of the relationship in which the communication takes place.

WHAT IS A COMMUNICATION CLIMATE?

A communication climate is the overarching sense of value and satisfaction individuals feel as they interact with each other and go about daily activities. While all marriages engage in roughly the same activities—dividing up household responsibilities, making ends meet, instructing and disciplining children, helping with endless homework, balancing work and home schedules, preparing for holidays, interacting with in-laws—the communication climate for each particular couple can greatly vary.

Some couples live in a perpetually chilly climate. They don't argue with each other, yet there is no warmth or intimacy between them. They go about their daily routines and never really connect. Other couples exist in a climate that is stormy and filled with arguments. These couples can't seem to agree on anything, and talking about issues only seems to make matters worse. Others live in a climate that is partly cloudy; communication is fine as long as certain topics—finances, sex, schedules—are avoided. Like rain clouds, these topics hang over a marriage and threaten to disrupt intimacy if they are discussed. And some couples seem to live in a state of never-ending sunshine. They seem to always be happy and affirming of one another, and they never utter a harsh word toward each other. The key for each of these couples is to understand how their climate formed and what it takes to maintain or alter it.

How you regularly interact with your spouse is the single greatest factor in establishing the communication climate that surrounds your marriage. It isn't "what we communicate about that shapes a relational climate, as much as *how* we speak and act toward one another," note the authors of *Interplay: The Process of Interpersonal Communication*.[1] The book of Proverbs forcefully states that both life and death reside in the tongue (see 18:21). Just as our speech can impart life and death, it also establishes the type of marital climate we experience every day.

While communication scholars agree that communication climates are vital to healthy relationships, not all scholars agree on the specific elements that make up a climate. While surveying journal articles, wading through current research, conducting my own research and speaking at marriage conferences for more than thirteen years, I've identified four key elements of a communication climate: acknowledgment, trust, expectations and commitment.[2] Each one of these elements warrants our attention.

ACKNOWLEDGMENT

Acknowledging another person is perhaps the most confirming form of communication and the most rare. We acknowledge another person when we take time to seek out and attend to his or her perspective. Acknowledgment is often expressed by eye contact, touching, asking questions and allowing the person to speak uninterrupted. Philosopher William James once said that the worst punishment he could think of was to exist in a community yet be unnoticed by others.

Acknowledging another person's perspective does not mean that we necessarily condone or agree with it. Rather, we simply recognize the validity and uniqueness of that perspective. To notice and engage another person as unique and irreplaceable is a deeply encouraging form of interaction.

The Jewish philosopher Martin Buber identified three broad ways we recognize and interact with others.[3] In an *I-It* relationship we do not even acknowledge or recognize the humanity of a person. When individuals walk out of a coffee shop and ignore the pleas of a homeless person asking for spare change, an I-It relationship is established. *I-You* relationships are formed when we acknowledge the humanity of people, but engage them only according to their social role, or what they can do for us. The people who serve us lunch at the cafeteria, garbage collectors, casual work associates, mail carriers and bus drivers can easily be placed into this category. To foster an *I-Thou* relationship with a person is to view him as unique and irreplaceable. These are rare relationships in which we acknowledge and focus on that person's qualities that no one else possesses.

When you first started dating your spouse, most likely this is what you felt when you were with him or her. You felt special and that you had your spouse's undivided attention. Early in the marriage your positive qualities were consistently acknowledged by your spouse, resulting in a positive communication climate. However, over the years, you may have slowly slipped into an I-You relationship, coming to see your partner only in his or her role as a husband or wife.

In the movie *Revolutionary Road*, Kate Winslet plays a woman who falls in love and marries a man (Leonardo DiCaprio) she describes as the "most interesting person she's ever met." She acknowledges his unique traits and is swept away by them. Yet, over time, her estimation of him fades as she gradually comes to view him merely as a husband, salesman and provider. Every day he gets up, showers, dresses in a charcoal suit and leaves for a ten-hour workday. He dispassionately serves his role as husband and father, as she serves her role as dutiful wife and mother. If we are not careful, we can do the same. When we take our spouse for granted, not only do we stop acknowledging him or her, but we also see that person as someone serving a predictable, useful role.

To counteract this slip into I-You relationships, we need to remember that each person with whom we come in contact— from those who deliver our mail to our spouse—carries the *imago Dei*—the image of God. Of all the creatures God created, we carry a unique likeness of God and represent him as image bearers. In light of this theological truth, we should seek to un-cover and acknowledge how each person, especially our spouse, uniquely reflects God's image. As theologian and popular author Eugene Peterson states, "There are no dittos among souls."[4]

TRUST

With regularity, media report on politicians, clergy, sports fig-ures and presidents being caught in lies. Young athletes have grown up in the steroids era and now look at sports heroes with a suspecting eye. The cumulative result of this chronic lack of trust is that we are encouraged "to interpret daily communica-tion actions from a vantage point of mistrust and doubt." If the communication climate between two people is marked by mistrust, a person "begins to question what is stated and looks for an unstated real answer, which begins a cycle of distrust and suspicion."[5]

This cycle of distrust was evident in a couple I once met at a marriage conference. During a break, the husband approached me and said that, early in the marriage, he had repeatedly lied to his wife about his addiction to pornography, and now his wife no longer trusted him and wanted out of the marriage. As we were talking, the wife walked up. She confirmed both his story and her desire to call it quits. She explained that, even though he'd broken free of pornography, she doubted whether she could trust him again. "To be honest," she concluded, "I've become suspicious of everything he tells me."

In marriage, we trust our spouse to follow through on promises, to keep his or her word and to protect our welfare. Trust is slowly built over time and, once ruptured, takes time and concerted effort to rebuild. Until that trust is built back up, the communication climate suffers.

If a lack of trust exists between individuals, any attempt to communicate effectively or to resolve differences will be compromised. For this reason the apostle Paul writes to the believers at Ephesus that they should "put off falsehood and speak truthfully" to others (Ephesians 4:25). He reminds the church at Colosse that, since they have taken off the old self, they should "not lie to each other" (Colossians 3:9).

The book of Proverbs presents the value of truthfulness, contrasting honesty with lying. In a nod to the Persian custom of trusted friends greeting each other with a kiss, one proverb states that an "honest answer is like a kiss on the lips" (24:26). Lying should be avoided not only because through it trust is destroyed, but also because a lying tongue both hurts and hates the recipient of the lie (see 26:28). Researchers continually identify trust as a foundational characteristic of healthy communication climates and relationships.[6]

EXPECTATIONS

On the day you said "I do," you married not only a person but also all his or her expectations of what marriage would be like. Words and phrases like *husband, wife, breadwinner, nurturer, spiritual leader, handyman, housekeeper, provider and cook* are all highly personalized concepts. Where did your ideas and definitions of these words come from?

The earliest and most lasting definitions you received came from your parents. In my wife's family, to be a husband meant that you were good with finances, fixed anything that broke around the house and had a knack for sales. In contrast, my father spent his entire life working on the assembly line at General Motors. When he came home, he was tired and wanted to relax. He was not interested in home becoming a second job. Consequently, when things broke around the house, they stayed broken.

See the problem? What happens when two married people have drastically different definitions of what it means to be "the man of the house"? I'll never forget the first time my wife called and said our van wouldn't start. I responded, "Bummer." I was a communication major in college; we didn't take courses on automotive care. What was I supposed to do?

A friend of mine who writes on marriage tells couples that in the midst of a disagreement, they need to ask, "Who's in the room with you?" He doesn't mean just your spouse. He means those who have influenced your view of marriage, roles, responsibilities and expectations. In short, who's whispering in your ear as you disagree over whose responsibility it is to fix the van?

This idea of who's in the room with you during an argument is vividly portrayed in the movie *The Story of Us*. In one scene, the couple is lying in bed, having an argument. Creatively, the director places each set of parents on opposite sides of the bed. During the argument, the mother whispers something into her daughter's ear. You can imagine what she's saying: "If he were a real man like your father he would provide for you better." The opposing father quickly counters and whispers to his son, "She needs to start appreciating all you do for her and the kids."

Your parents unknowingly helped to create the *constitutive rules* of communication that greatly influence how you interact. Constitutive rules are created by couples to express what counts as respect, love, support, disrespect, connection and commitment in the relationship. These rules, while deeply influenced by family members and culture, are highly individualistic to each couple. For Noreen, a key constitutive rule is that support is expressed by initiating help around the house. For her, to have to ask me to help empty the dishwasher or help the kids with homework is interpreted as me taking her for granted (also a constitutive rule).

My constitutive rule for support is Noreen's willingness to read rough drafts of articles or to take an interest in my creative projects. Taking time to learn what counts as *attentiveness* (such as not interrupting), *respect* (such as not disagreeing with each other in public), *responsibility* (such as paying bills on time), *spirituality* (such as praying regularly as a couple), *intimacy* (such as holding hands in public), *romance* (such as going to dinner) and so on, will greatly add to the health of your communication climate.

Be warned: learning the constitutive rules of your spouse is only half the battle. To learn what my wife counts as romance (planning a date and arranging for a sitter) but never following through on it will also cause a chill in our climate.

COMMITMENT

In a culture described as "the divorce culture," the health of a couple's communication climate hinges on commitment and mutual investment. "The hallmark of commitment," notes relationship expert Julia Wood, is "the assumption of a future."[7] Psychologists have long noted how commitment between individuals fosters feelings of empowerment and positive self-image. In one study, individuals who felt a secure bond to their spouses were given a list of adjectives to describe themselves. The more connected an individual felt to his or her spouse, the more positive the trait he or she picked out. These same individuals readily admitted that they didn't live up to all their ideals but still felt good about themselves based on the overall security of their relationship.[8]

Security and oneness are at the heart of the Genesis account of God's intention for marriage: "Therefore a man leaves his father and his mother and cleaves to his wife, and they become one flesh" (Genesis 2:24 RSV).

A man leaves his father and his mother. In some African tribes, the entire village dances along with a newly married couple as they leave the village, according to Tim Stafford in *A Love Story*. "There is no license, no piece of paper. The village is present to show its support and reinforce responsibility to the partner, to any potential children, and to society."[9] When I married Noreen, I transitioned from primarily being the son of John and Nancy Muehlhoff to primarily being the husband of Noreen Muehlhoff. She became my chief concern.

And cleaves to his wife. What does it mean to cleave? Stafford explains that to cleave means a husband and wife stick to one another like two pieces of paper glued together. The individual sheets cannot be separated without significant tearing and damage. Cleaving is the decision to share everything: time, money, emotions, thoughts, fears, failures and triumphs.

And "become one flesh." For all our clamoring for independence and freedom, most of us want to be stuck with someone. The result of uniting our soul to another is that we become one with that person—spiritually, intellectually, emotionally and physically. The relationship described in Genesis should stop us in our tracks when we read it. It is asking us to make the decision to leave the security of our family and to commit entirely to one person to face a lifetime of unforeseen challenges. A friend of mine, paralyzed by the thought of getting engaged, asked a popular speaker on relationships what one question he should ask himself when considering marriage. The speaker surprised him with this simple question: "Do you want to eat breakfast with this person for the rest of your life?" In other words, was he willing to be with this person at the start and end of every day for the next sixty years?

This assumption of a future together is what helps a couple get past what communication scholars call "the inevitability of conflict." Studies focusing on conflict have centered on relationships between college students, family members, coworkers, friends, dating partners and spouses, to name a few. Their general conclusion is that conflict is common and inevitable to all relationships. What surprises many Christian couples is that simply being followers of Christ does not exempt them from conflict.

Even though Paul exhorts the Philippians to "make my joy complete by being like-minded" and be "one in spirit and purpose" (Philippians 2:2), he still has to intervene in a disagreement between Euodia and Syntyche and ask them to "agree with each other in the Lord" (4:2). Paul tells believers at Corinth that they have been called to be holy "together with all those everywhere who call on the name of our Lord Jesus Christ" (1 Corinthians 1:2). Yet, nine verses later, he writes that he has learned there are "quarrels among you" (v. 11). Paul himself experienced conflict with Peter over Peter's decision to separate from Gentile Christians and eat only with Jewish Christians (see Galatians 2:11-14).

Just as Christian communities struggle with the inevitability of conflict, so do Christian marriages. However, what helps believers get through marital conflict is knowing that you and your spouse are in it for the long haul. Once, during a heated argument, Noreen said to me, "We need to figure this out now, or the next fifty years are going to be exhausting." The subtext was clear: "I'm not going anywhere, so let's get to work." Similarly, I have a friend who tells his wife, "If you leave me, I'll follow you."

Contrast those attitudes with that of a former professor of mine who taught on relationships. He regularly told us that the only way a couple can survive the stress and pressure of marriage is to have a back door to the marriage. Knowing that you can exit the marriage if it gets too demanding or difficult, according to his view, takes the pressure off and gives you courage to face difficulties in the here and now. Such an attitude stands in stark contrast to the one-flesh approach to marriage poetically described in the Scriptures.

For your communication climate to become positive and nurturing, there cannot be a preplanned exit strategy. Your marital climate will always suffer if you carry a nagging doubt that if the relationship gets too messy or difficult, your partner will leave. In contrast, the mere fact that you know that your spouse, though not perfect, is committed to you, will create an atmosphere for a healthy climate.

THINK IT OVER

1. What can you do regularly to foster an I-Thou relationship

with your spouse and communicate that he is special and
unique? How do couples slowly take each other for granted
and slip into an I-You relationship?

2. If a lack of trust exists between individuals, any attempt to
effectively resolve differences will be compromised. Do you
feel your spouse is a person of her word? When engaged in a
disagreement with your spouse, do you trust him not to use
your words against you?

3. Which two or three individuals have most influenced your
view of marriage, marital roles, responsibilities and expectations? In other words, when discussing marriage with
your spouse, who's in the room with you, whispering in
your ear?

4. Psychologists have long noted how commitment between individuals fosters a positive self-image. How has being married to your spouse influenced how you see yourself and
formed your general sense of who you are today?

Environmental Press

Why Marriage Can Be a Struggle

*F*or twelve months Jennifer meticulously planned her wedding. The dress was perfect, outdoor patio decorated, bridesmaids in position, guests seated and a four-course dinner waiting. Everything was going according to plan. Everything except the one factor she couldn't control—the climate.

During the outdoor ceremony, small flecks of ash, white like confetti, fell on her dress. Helicopters noisily swooped above her on their way to drop tons of water on a raging fire. The California wildfires that ravaged thousands of acres and hundreds of homes in the summer of 2007 were visible on the horizon. Jennifer's wedding fell one mile outside the mandatory evacuation zone. In addition to guests, a minister and family members, two firefighters stood in the back, listening to reports from the Fire Authority through earpieces. If the wind shifted suddenly, the wedding would be called off and guests evacuated. After a drizzle started to fall during the reception, Jennifer commented that every element—wind, fire, rain—had showed up for the wedding.

This couple's precarious wedding during wildfire season reflects marriage climates everywhere. Marriage counselors use the term "environmental press" to describe how culture presses in on all marriages, making them a struggle. Just as Jennifer had to deal with fire, rain and swirling ash, marriages must contend with equally threatening elements. Jennifer's advantage? She could see what was coming.

The social climate surrounding our marriages, though invisible, poses threats whose effects on a relationship are equal to a wildfire. From the moment you say "I do," today's culture puts enormous pressure on you and your spouse. Culture encompasses the rules, definitions, behaviors and beliefs that were handed to you as a child. Culture is a set of definitions that tell you not only what to value in life but also how to live in a way that is acceptable in your particular society.

We feel pressure to conform to our culture's view of four powerful elements: time, status, romance and the prevalence of divorce. It's not enough just to recognize these pressures; we also need to understand how they influence our marital climate.

HURRYSICKNESS

In the morning you hurriedly gulp a cup of coffee and devour a breakfast bar as you read and respond to a dozen emails. You barely say a word to your spouse in the mad dash to make and clean up breakfast, pack lunches and drop the kids off at school before 8:30. During lunch, you eat an energy bar as you try to squeeze in a workout *and* drop off pictures for one-hour processing *and* pick up clothes from the cleaner. When the kids come home from school, the day really picks up. Two of them have soccer practice while the third has ballet. You eat fast food in the van as you drive to three different locations. In the evening, after helping with science and math projects, paying bills, responding to more email, checking Facebook and sifting through junk mail, you reintroduce yourself to your spouse as you collapse into bed. You barely say a word to each other as you drift off listening to the news on CNN.

Does this day sound familiar? Experts describe this lifestyle as *hurrysickness*.[1] Hurrysickness results from living in a constant state of overdrive, cramming each moment so full of events that we have no time to experience them in any meaningful way. This chronic hurry is characterized by the need to continually accomplish multiple tasks at once. Our addiction to hurriedness and efficiency comes at an unexpected price. "We have quickened the pace of life only to become less patient. We have become more organized and less spontaneous, less joyful," says Jeremy Rifkin in his book *Time Wars: The Primary Conflict in Human History*.[2]

In April 2007, staff members at the *Washington Post* wanted to see if people would slow down long enough to enjoy an impromptu performance by a world-class artist. To carry out their experiment, they dressed internationally acclaimed violin virtuoso Joshua Bell in jeans, a T-shirt and a ball cap, and had him play a 3.5-million-dollar violin in the middle of the D.C. metro rush hour. Surely even hurrysick individuals would stop to hear classics played to perfection at no cost.

Bell started at 7:51 a.m. and played six classical pieces as precisely 1,097 people passed by. A video recording of the event shows only a handful of people turning toward the music and only occasional stragglers stopping to listen.

The organizers were shocked; they had actually made contingency plans for handling a crowd. When people were asked by staffers why they didn't stop, the most common answers were that they were in a hurry, had other things on their mind or just didn't notice. One man, when asked why he didn't even acknowledge Bell, was shocked to learn that he had stood a mere four feet away from him.[3]

How does hurrysickness affect your marital climate? Significant communication rarely occurs between hurried individuals. Acknowledgment is a key part of a communication climate, but in a hurrysick world, we simply don't have time to acknowledge each other. Aside from logistical communication ("When is Tommy's soccer game?" "Don't forget, you have a doctor's appointment this afternoon." "Karen's science project is due tomorrow.") how much time do we take each day to focus on each other and engage in interpersonal communication?[4]

This question was so pressing to our friends across the pond that it spurred a national survey. British researchers from the Office for National Statistics (ONS) found that the average British couple spent just fifteen minutes a day engaging each other or enjoying a social life together. Through looking at 21,000 daily dairies and 11,700 interviews, researchers concluded that most couples spent the majority of their time away from each other—mainly due to work and kids—and, when together, would do housework, sleep or watch television, which the ONS identified as a passive activity that *inhibited* interaction. The ONS noted that weekends were merely times to catch up on sleep and watch *more* television. One psychotherapist, commenting on the results, concluded: "You can't have a relationship if you don't see the other person."[5]

As I consider the crazy schedule of the Muehlhoff family and those around me, I think American couples easily mirror the results of our British counterparts. Along with British researchers, those studying American couples have long noted that children can often become the focal point of a marriage. Research shows that marital satisfaction tends to steadily decline as children are added to the mix.[6] Why? If we are not careful, we can spend less and less time engaging each other and pour all of our time into acknowledging the kids.

Proverbs 20:5 says that the "purposes of a [person's] heart

are deep waters" and that only through time and careful prodding can we "draw them out," to use the language of that proverb. Drawing out the thoughts and feelings of another requires what psychologist Gerald Egan calls total listening: "Total listening is more than attending to another person's words. It is also listening to the meanings that are buried in the words and between the words and in the silences in communication."[7] As hurrysick individuals, we may desire to listen and draw our spouse out in a way described by Egan, but we live in a way that makes it almost impossible to accomplish. "We are a nation that shouts at a microwave to hurry up," notes columnist Joan Ryan.[8] If we won't slow down long enough even to acknowledge a world-class violinist, will we slow down enough to listen to the seemingly mundane perspective of our spouse or children?

Our time and energy disappear because of another cultural element that presses against our marriages: our desire to keep up with the Joneses—literally.

Affluenza

"We spend money we don't have to buy things we don't need to impress people we don't like," Woody Allen observed. In 2001, an economics professor, an environmental watchdog and an award-winning television producer set out to see if Allen's humorous insight was true: do Americans purchase things to feel better about themselves and to impress others?

After carefully examining our frantic American lifestyle, they diagnosed us with a disease they creatively call "affluenza." Affluenza is a "painful, contagious, socially transmitted condition of overload, debt, anxiety and waste resulting in the dogged pursuit of more."[9] Like many diseases, it can be detected only by its symptoms. The presence of affluenza becomes obvious when we consider what we value, how we spend our time and our level of contentment in the midst of it all. The diagnosis is not encouraging.

In each of the past four years more Americans declared personal bankruptcy than graduated from college. Our annual production of solid waste would fill a convoy of garbage trucks stretching halfway to the moon. We have twice as many shopping centers as high schools. We now work more hours each year than do the citizens of any other industrial country, including Japan. Ninety-five percent of our workers say they wish they could spend more time with their families.[10]

"We spend money we don't have to buy things we don't need to impress people we don't like." Columnist Ellen Goodman describes what this obsession costs us on a day-to-day basis. The day starts "getting dressed in clothes that you buy for work, driving through traffic in a car that you are still paying for, in order to get to the job that you need so you can pay for the clothes, car and the house that you leave empty all day in order to afford to live in it."[11]

How does affluenza affect your marital climate? Affluenza breeds dissatisfaction. Every time I connect to the Internet, I'm met by a pop-up window that tells me my Internet connection could be twice as fast. Our family van is fine, but TV ads remind me that it doesn't have OnStar or built-in DVD players. Even before I had figured out how to use my new laptop computer, techno-savvy friends were telling me if I bought the same computer today it would have a bigger screen, a super-thin DVD burner, three times the memory and an integrated optical drive. In an age of affluenza, we are taught to be dissatisfied, to focus on what we *don't* have.

This conditioned dissatisfaction bleeds over into our marriages. If we're not careful, over time the same dissatisfaction we can have with a year-old personal computer can be true of how we view our spouse. We start to take note of the qualities our spouse doesn't have.

Affluenza also fosters isolation. Our homes have become cocoons where we cut ourselves off from neighbors and even from each other. Mom is watching a new DVD in the living room. Dad is on the Internet, checking out the latest scores. Brother and sister are upstairs in separate rooms, playing two different games on two different PSPs. Glenn Stanton, a director of a family-support organization, calls this phenomenon "the new homelessness": "Everybody is connected to something outside the home even though they are physically within the home."[12] The effects are obvious: less time together, less time to communicate.

Affluenza also threatens the most important part of our communication climate: trust. When so much time and energy is spent doggedly pursing more, we start to lose trust that *we* are more important than status and things. On our wedding day, we made a promise in front of friends, family, our lover and God that our marriage would be primary above all else. Now, in an age of affluenza, we are in danger of breaking our word and the trust our spouse had in us.

When we finally do carve out time to discuss key issues in our marriage, the unrealistic expectations we have of each other often fuel frustration.

AN OVERLY ROMANTIC VIEW OF LOVE AND MARRIAGE
A fascinating study done by relationship experts at Heriot-Watt University in Edinburgh sought to determine if romantic comedies influence how we view love, sex and marriage.[13] They specifically examined forty box-office hits between 1995 and 2005, such as *Runaway Bride*, *Notting Hill*, *You've Got Mail*, *Maid in Manhattan* and *While You Were Sleeping*.

One hundred volunteers watched romantic comedies and then

discussed their view of love and romance. Researchers concluded that these movies could easily "spoil your love life" by fostering unrealistic ideas of love, such as believing fate brings individuals together and that a soul mate will anticipate your deepest needs without you having to voice them. Researcher Kimberly Johnson offered this assessment: "Films do capture the excitement of new relationships but they also wrongly suggest that trust and committed love exists from the moment people meet, whereas these are qualities that normally take years to develop."[14]

Other relationship experts agree and suggest that, through much trial and error, it takes couples on the average nine to fourteen years to find a rhythm in their relationship.[15] Such information helps us adjust our expectations and take a long view of our relationship, knowing that it takes years—and many struggles—to adjust to married life and work out relational kinks. Couples who call it quits in the first seven years of marriage—the average for couples divorcing in the United States—are simply not giving themselves enough time to develop a healthy marital climate.

How does an overly romantic view of love affect your marital climate? A prototype is the clearest example of a category. We all have prototypes of the perfect date, the perfect job, the perfect car, the perfect romantic evening, the perfect marriage. We also have a prototype of romantic love. When I ask my students at the university where I teach to describe the person they want to marry and love for the rest of their life, they give the following general description: a person who will *always* care for me, *always* look out for me, *always* accept me, *always* pursue me, *always* be interested in me . . . Perfectly consistent love—one that isn't subject to good and bad days—can be found only in the Scriptures. To expect our spouse to love, pursue or understand us as only God can is unrealistic and sure to cause frustration and profound disappointment. Only one being can love you perfectly: God. As we will consider in chapter twelve, only after experiencing God's unwavering love can you be satisfied with frail human love.

The last element that presses against our marriages is the strongest and most damaging.

Divorce Culture and Starter Marriages

When it comes to love and commitment, the message we get from society is clear: nothing lasts forever.

Love, as presented in films, novels and music, is a powerful emotion that ebbs and flows and eventually flames out. Sometimes this flameout happens staggeringly quickly. Through Letterman and Leno and TMZ, we are brought up to date on short-lived celebrity marriages: pop princess Britney Spears and actor Jason Alexander (55 hours), model Carmen Electra and ex-pro basketball player Dennis Rodman (9 days), Drew Barrymore and Jeremy Thomas (19 days), Jennifer Lopez and former backup dancer Cris Judd (8 months), tennis great Chris Evert and professional golfer Greg Norman (15 months) and so on. After separating from his wife after eight days, actor Dennis Hopper said, "Seven of the days were pretty good. It was the eighth day that was the bad one."[16] Every day we inhale the cultural message that love is ambiguous, flimsy and unstable.

High-school students apparently have been deeply influenced by the Britney Spearses of the world, as evidenced in how they now refer to marriage. A first marriage is often described as a "starter marriage." Just as you buy a starter home with the idea of moving on to something bigger and better, so teens also view a first marriage. While they don't plan to divorce, they view a first marriage as a possible stepping stone to a hopefully more lasting marriage.

Can we blame them?

Divorce has become a tragically common occurrence. On my

son's soccer team, three couples divorced in one year. Half of the kids in the church Bible study I lead come from broken families. A friend of mind recently mentioned a website that sells miniature coffins for a person desiring to bury not only a failing relationship but his or her wedding ring as well. The site reads, "Give a dead marriage its proper, final resting place. The Wedding Ring Coffin is the perfect gift for yourself."[17]

How does the divorce culture affect your marital climate? The fear that your marriage may not make it poses the greatest threat to your marital climate. While all couples experience struggles during marriage, there's a significant difference between being secure in the relationship as you face struggles and being worried that difficulties could end the marriage. In light of today's sober statistics concerning divorce, many couples live with the unspoken fear that their marriage will not make it.

Tragically, many couples within the Christian community also live with this fear. According to research from the Barna Group, Christians are less likely to live together before marriage but just as likely to divorce as non-Christians. The study reports that 33 percent of all born-again Christians have gone through a divorce, which is statistically identical to the divorce rate among non-born-again adults (34 percent).[18] The Barna Group concludes that in America the institution of marriage is not as stable as it once was. Unfortunately, that appears to apply equally for those inside and outside the Christian community.

The Scriptures take a dramatically different view of love and commitment and call us to a higher standard. In the Song of Solomon, Solomon's bride exclaims, "Love is as strong as death" (8:6). If we want to create healthy marital climates, we need to reverse the disturbing trend reported by Barna and embrace this biblical view of love.

One of the reasons Jennifer pulled off her unlikely wedding in the face of raging California wildfires was that she and her guests knew what they were facing. Receiving constant weather reports and seeing the red glow on the horizon allowed them to make plans to counteract a hostile climate. The more we understand how the cultural climate surrounding our marriages presses in on us and threatens to hinder our intimacy, the more we can, like Jennifer, make plans to counter those challenges. All followers of Christ are urged to resist the temptation to conform to the seductive and powerful patterns of this world (see Romans 12:1-2).

THINK IT OVER

1. Rank the four elements you've just read about—hurriedness, affluenza, overly romantic view of love, prevalence of divorce—according to how they press on and affect the climate of your marriage.

2. British couples only spend an average of fifteen minutes a day engaging each other. How much time do you spend a day focusing on each other that is not spent in front of the television or centering on the kids? When do you find is the best time to grab some time for yourselves and perhaps talk to each other about personal issues (after dinner, before bed, when the kids go to bed)? When is the least effective time (before dinner, when one of you walks through the door from work, when you know your favorite shows are on)?

3. Woody Allen quipped, "We spend money we don't have to buy things we don't need to impress people we don't like." What effect do finances, debt and keeping up with the neighbors have on the climate of your marriage?

4. How much has Hollywood's portrayal of romance spoiled our view of love or shaped our expectations of each other? Am I asking my spouse to love me in ways only God can?

Improving Your
Communication Climate

*I*f you watched the opening ceremony of the 2008 Summer Olympic Games in Beijing, you were one of 2 billion worldwide who witnessed a cast of 15,000 depicting Chinese history through dazzling fireworks and laser shows that lit up the sky over the National Stadium. Most of us huddled around television sets in awe of what we saw.

But it almost didn't happen. Two days before the opening ceremonies, the producers received the worst possible forecast: a 90-percent chance of rain coupled with lightning. A massive rain belt was moving toward the stadium that would make fireworks and a laser show impossible. What could be done?

In a daring move, meteorologists fired more than one thousand rain dispersal rockets from twenty-one sites around the city to intercept the rain and push it away. Sound crazy? On the night of the opening ceremonies, the skies were clear and the celebration breathtaking.[1]

The lesson to be taken from the organizers of the Twenty-Ninth Olympiad is that of planning. Instead of wringing their hands and hoping the storm clouds would pass by or the forecasters had gotten it wrong, the producers came up with a plan to change the climate. We would do well to do the same. Many couples, when faced with a stormy climate, ignore it and hope that things will get better. Sometimes they do; often they don't. Marriage forecasting is about adopting a different course of action; it's about setting out intentionally to alter the communication climate of your marriage. The following three chapters will help you focus on and strengthen the climate between you and your spouse.

Remember that every communication climate is made up of four elements: acknowledgment, expectations, commitment and trust. The key to improving marriage is not just being aware of these factors, but learning how to strengthen them. Just as the Chinese sent up all those rockets to push away the ongoing storm, we'll strategically target the acknowledgment, commitment and expectation components of a communication climate.

STRENGTHENING ACKNOWLEDGMENT: BEING MINDFUL

The communication climate with your spouse will grow more positive when you take time to seek out and attend to your spouse's perspective. That is no small accomplishment in our fast-paced, hurrysick world. The first step in improving your ability to acknowledge your spouse's perspective is to practice what communication experts call "mindfulness."

Mindfulness is the increasingly lost art of being fully present in the moment with all your attention focused in one direction or on one person. When I'm seeking to acknowledge your perspective, I'm not looking over your shoulder at news updates on the TV screen or checking text messages on my cell phone or thinking about my day or even being aware of what's going on around me.

One of my favorite sports movies is *For Love of the Game*. The movie centers on baseball legend Billy Chapel (played by Kevin Costner), who is pitching a no-hitter in his last professional game. As each batter comes up to the plate and goes down swinging, the crowd goes crazy, making it hard for Chapel to focus. To focus, he keeps telling himself to "clear the mechanism." In the novel that the movie is based on, it's described this way: "He put his foot on the rubber and the sound faded slowly away. He was no longer aware of the crowd. He saw no faces, no flags, heard no sound at all from the mass out there."[2]

While complete mindfulness is impossible (parents of toddlers, anyone?) it's useful to repeat to ourselves regularly "clear the mechanism" when we are trying to focus on and acknowledge the perspective of our spouse in the midst of a conversation. When my attention starts to slip, I'll silently say to myself "clear the mechanism" as many times as it takes to refocus on what Noreen is saying to me.

In addition to cultivating mindfulness, experts at the Harvard Negotiation Project maintain that acknowledging the feelings or perspectives of another person entails letting that person know three important things: First, let that person know that what he or she has shared with you has *made an impression on you*. The standard rule of acknowledgment is this: any reaction is better than *no* reaction. A wise marriage counselor once told me that the opposite of love is not hate, but indifference.

Second, acknowledging the feelings of another person means letting that person know that her or his *feelings matter to you*. A mistake we commonly make with our spouse is saying he or she shouldn't feel that way. One of the lessons I learned early in my marriage (after much trial and error) is that initial feelings are not necessarily right or wrong, they just *are*. When Noreen or the boys are upset, it is irrelevant for me to step in and determine if they *should* be upset. At the moment when a person first

expresses pain or disappointment, it is wise simply to acknowledge her or his hurt and emotion.

   The third suggestion from the experts at Harvard is to let the
person know that you are *working to understand what he or she
is saying.* "An acknowledgment is simply this: any indication
that you are struggling to understand the emotional content of
what the other person is saying."[3] This statement takes the
pressure off you to find the perfect response. When your spouse
finishes sharing her or his feelings, the appropriate way to acknowledge those feelings may be to (1) say nothing and simply
nod in agreement; (2) put back into your own words what your
spouse just said; (3) ask a clarifying question: "When you said
_____, what did you mean?"; (4) ask if there's anything
else he or she would like to add; (5) ask your spouse what she
or he needs from you right now; (6) offer to pray for your spouse.
The mere fact that you are working to acknowledge and attend
to the perspective of your spouse will strengthen the climate of
your marriage.

   Acknowledgment is not limited to what a person says, but
also recognizing what he or she does. A favorite saying of Dennis Rainey, founder and president of FamilyLife, is "Catch your
spouse doing what's right." We often are quick to do the opposite, aren't we? When our spouse messes up, we are there to
point it out, while regrettably slow to point out the positive. A
powerful way to strengthen your communication climate is to
acknowledge purposefully the positive things your spouse does
for you regularly.

   My wife and I notice that each time our marital climate starts
to deteriorate, it's due to a pervasive feeling that we have started
to take each other for granted. To remedy this, we have on oc-
casion agreed to set aside a week and not let a day end without
complimenting each other at least once. To be honest, whenever we do this, the first day is the most awkward. But once we

push through and the compliments start to pile up, the results are amazing. After one such week, I wrote down my list of compliments, put them in a frame and gave them to Noreen. Here's a sample:

> *Thank you* for washing, drying and folding the mountain of laundry produced daily by the Muehlhoff men.

> *Thanks* for keeping the pantry stocked for three boys who are *always* hungry.

> *Thanks* for helping Mike with high-school geometry that is way beyond this former communication major.

> I appreciated you offering to pick up Jason from a friend's house when I had just sat down to watch the start of *SportsCenter*.

> You are a great sports mom who never complains about going to a ridiculous number of Little League baseball games and sitting on stiff aluminum bleachers.

The odd thing about marriage is that the more familiar we become with each other, the less we say "thank you," "please" and "you're welcome." When Noreen and I take time to recognize each other and verbalize our appreciation, it doesn't take long for our climate to change for the better. Proverbs states that pleasant words are sweet and bring healing to a person's soul and body (see 16:24).

STRENGTHENING COMMITMENT: REMEMBERING THE PAST
AND INVESTING IN THE PRESENT

If commitment is lacking in a relationship, the marital climate will inevitably be unstable. The way to stabilize and strengthen commitment is to focus on past acts of commitment and then to continue to invest in the present.

According to marriage expert John Gottman, one of the key indicators of the strength of a couple's marriage and commitment is how that couple recalls their past. "Through my research on couples," he writes, "I have found that nothing foretells a marriage's future as accurately as how a couple retells their past."[4] Gottman discovered that when most couples look back on their history, they tend to focus on either a pervasive feeling of disappointment or a sense of pride in the struggles they have gone through. While all marriages go through ups and downs, men and women who are struggling or unhappy tend to dwell on times when the marriage was in crisis or when their spouse let them down. On the other hand, spouses in healthy marriages look back fondly at the past with a sense of pride that they have come through the fire and are still standing as a couple. Humorist Erma Bombeck looked back on her forty-plus years with her husband and wrote,

> We've gone through three wars, two miscarriages, five houses, three children, 17 cars, 23 funerals, seven camping trips, 12 jobs, 19 banks and three credit unions. I stopped counting slammed doors after 3,009. What do I have to show for it? A feeling of pride and contentment for having done something that isn't easy.[5]

Going through two miscarriages, 23 funerals and countless arguments evidenced by thousands of slammed doors is not fun. No doubt there was a lot of pain in the numbers and situations listed by Bombeck. But, there is also a lot of joy and pride.

While Noreen and I have not gone through nearly what Erma and her husband did, we have our own growing list of struggles. When our firstborn son, Michael, was six weeks old, I went into the nursery to change his diaper. When I turned on the light, I was shocked to see him covered in spit-up mixed with blood. Noreen and I hurriedly rushed him to the emer-

gency room, where we were told he had pyloric stenosis—
blockage that wouldn't allow food to pass out of his stomach—
and would require an operation within the hour. While that
surgery was a fairly simple procedure, it's always risky to put a
newborn under anesthesia.

Well, as first-time parents we were a mess. After calling family and friends, we sat, held hands, cried and prayed. To this
day, when we see our seventeen-year-old run around with his
shirt off and see that tiny scar, we think back to the waiting
room and that small slice of our marital history.

What's your history? One of the important ways to strengthen
commitment is to remember key moments of your past. When
Noreen and I recently celebrated our nineteenth wedding anniversary, we walked along a beach and went year by year, trying to remember key events that happened in our marriage that
shaped us. Some of the events made us laugh; others were so-
bering to reflect on. We also tried to see where God had been
moving in our marriage and family and where he might be
moving now. The Scriptures state that spiritual reflection is one
the most important disciplines we can cultivate. In Psalm 77
David wrote, "I will remember the deeds of the LORD; yes, I will
remember your miracles of long ago" (v. 11). As couples, we
would do well to become attentive to what Christian author
Gary Thomas calls the "sacred history" God is cultivating in
each of our marriages.

At the end of this chapter, you'll be asked to reflect on key
moments of your "sacred history," such as when you first met,
your first kiss, getting engaged, the birth of a child, the purchase of your first car, the first church you attended as a couple,
anniversaries and so on. As couples we would do well to record
these key moments in a journal or couple's diary. As time goes
by, memories fade and the significance of times, places and
events lose their power.

Soon after we got married, Noreen and I started the habit of purchasing Christmas ornaments from the places we visited, to serve as reminders. We have a miniature streetcar from a weekend business trip to San Francisco and a glass replica of Mt. Rushmore from a family vacation and so on, combined with ornaments the boys made in church and elementary school. Each Christmas as we decorate the tree, we are reminded of events and seasons of life long forgotten.

Recorded events and artifacts will serve as a powerful reminder of the investments that would be lost if your marriage ended. Relationship expert Julia Wood says, "We can't get back the time, feelings, and energy we invest in a relationship. We cannot recover the history we have shared with another person. Thus, to leave is to lose the investment we have made."[6]

If you are currently in a difficult place in your marriage, know that your perseverance greatly pleases God. Gary Thomas argues that when we decide to hold firm to our commitment to our spouse through difficult times, we come to understand not only God's purpose for marriage, but his character as well. In fact, he writes, "marriage helps us develop the character of God himself as we stick with our spouses through the good times and the bad. Every wedding gives birth to a new history, a new beginning. The spiritual meaning of marriage is found in maintaining that history together."[7] Those of you who remain faithful to each other in the midst of difficulties will experience a depth of God's love that can come only through perseverance and dependence on God.

At many of the marriage conferences where I speak, I often have a spouse come up to me and say, "We aren't doing well in our marriage. Pray for us." I tell them I will pray. But I also tell them to be encouraged that they are there together. "I know of a lot of couples who are not doing well in their marriage, but they are not here. You are." When couples like these reflect on the history of their marriage, taking a weekend to fight for their marriage should be noted and celebrated.

INVESTING IN THE PRESENT

Commitment is not only strengthened by focusing on past investments but by continuing to invest in your marriage daily. One of the difficulties couples run into is that a spouse will feel the marriage has become a one-way street where he or she is investing more than the spouse. "When we feel we are investing more than a partner, we tend to be dissatisfied and resentful," Wood writes. "When it seems our partner is investing more than we are, we may feel guilty."[8] Generally, *investments* are seen as the time, energy, thoughts and feelings we put into a relationship. The key to building commitment is to value the different ways we invest or put energy into the relationship. For example, while both a husband and wife would view carving out time in today's hurrysick world to connect with each other as a significant relational investment, there might be disagreement as to what constitutes connection.

One of my wife's favorite things to do with her girlfriends is to grab coffee and talk. "Women discuss not only major events and issues but also day-to-day activities," Wood writes. "This small talk isn't really small at all, because it allows friends to understand the rhythms of each other's lives."[9] For many women, face-to-face conversations are one of the key ways they invest in relationships. Georgetown University linguist and relationship author Deborah Tannen calls this type of communication between women "rapport-talk," where individuals seek to establish connection through matching experiences and pointing out similarities.[10] Consequently, women may view their husband's attempt to engage them in conversation and to acknowledge or match their experiences as an investment in the marriage.

While men are not averse to face-to-face conversations with

their spouse, it's not the primary way men connect or the most important relational investment. Men often find it easier and more meaningful to establish closeness through sharing in a common activity or goal. Through the activity, men bond and gradually open up and express themselves. C. S. Lewis expressed a male orientation to connection when he wrote that it "is when we are doing things together that friendship springs up—painting, sailing, praying, philosophizing, fighting shoulder to shoulder."[11]

I often discuss marriage, spirituality, parenting and life aspirations with one of my closest male friends, Jon, but we seldom just sit and talk. Our closeness developed on the tennis court, fighting for every point. Even though both of us would call ourselves Christian, an occasional racket flies toward the fence. In the midst of playing tennis, we find time to talk about theology, politics, kids, marriage and life. Some days, when we don't have much time, talk is kept to a minimum as we play a quick set; we know the activity is the investment in the relationship. Men tend to regard their marital climate as positive if their wife invests in the relationship by joining them in common activities.

Because men and women tend to view relational investments and connection differently, a husband and wife need to give preference to each other. Some days, I invest in our marriage by calling Noreen and asking her out to lunch, where we sit across from each other and catch up on the day's events. In turn, Noreen invests by sitting with me and watching a hockey game and rooting on my favorite team, the beloved Detroit Red Wings. Much like our financial investments, our relational investments strengthen over time.

EXPECTATIONS: LOWERING EXPECTATIONS AND GETTING THEM OUT IN THE OPEN

From the moment you and your significant other started to realize marriage could be a reality, expectations started to ma-

terialize and hover around you. The extent to which those expectations or future expectations are met or unmet goes a long
way in determining the climate of your marriage. The first step
in addressing expectations is to determine if you need to lower
the expectations you place on your spouse.

Lowering expectations. Clinical psychologist Sue Johnson
observed that a majority of her clients live in a community of
two: them and their spouse. "Most of us no longer live in supportive communities with our birth families or childhood
friends close at hand. We work longer hours, commute farther
and farther distances, and thus have fewer and fewer opportunities to develop close relationships." After years of counseling
couples, her conclusion is, "We now ask our lovers for the emotional connection and sense of belonging that my grandmother
could get from a whole village."[12] Asking your spouse to meet
all your emotional or relational needs eliminates the need you
have to be part of a dynamic collective of believers that reflects
the love and unity of Christ.

As followers of Christ, we need to remember that God calls
us into relationship not just with our spouse but also with
members of his church. Our decision to follow Christ is also a
decision to form relationships with fellow believers. The apostle Paul's favorite metaphor for this community of believers is
the human body: "Now you are the body of Christ, and each of
you is a part of it" (1 Corinthians 12:27). His image of a body
implies a vital relational interconnectedness between those of
us who make up Christ's body. Paul states that we are "held
together by every supporting ligament" and that, when we take
time to care for and nurture each other, the whole body will
grow in love as "each part does its work" (Ephesians 4:16).
God's desire is that our interconnectedness be so tangible that
when one of us experiences disappointment or joy, we all would
know it and respond accordingly. "If one part suffers," he writes,

"every part suffers with it; if one part is honored, every part rejoices with it" (1 Corinthians 12:26). The body of Christ becomes the perfect place to put into practice Paul's exhortation to consider others before ourselves (see Philippians 2:3).

Noreen and I know that our marriage has been greatly deepened by being involved in both a church and a couples' Bible study with three other families, where we celebrate life together and help each other through life's struggles. Because this body of believers helps meet my personal and spiritual needs, I don't place unrealistic expectations on Noreen to constantly attend to me. Being part of this community also gives us a common goal: to be agents of grace to other couples or families God has brought across our path.

Discuss your expectations. The next step in managing expectations is to get them out in the open. The interesting thing about expectations is that we usually don't know we have them until they aren't met. Noreen and I have encountered the expectation trap in two unexpected contexts: lazy fall afternoons and birthday cards.

As soon as the clock hit 1:00 p.m. on the first Saturday afternoon of the college football season, I did what I always did: grabbed a soda and a bag of chips, moved the recliner in front of the TV and turned on football. I'd been doing that as long as I can remember. Some of my earliest and fondest memories were watching the University of Michigan Wolverines beat the *hated* Ohio State Buckeyes or the *despised* fighting Irish of Notre Dame. I often watched this glorious gridiron beat-down with my father and two older brothers.

Just as the kickoff was about to start, Noreen walked in and said, "I'm going to do some yard work. Want to help?"

Without looking up, I said, "You're kidding, right?"

She responded, "Tim, you're not going to sit here all day and watch a game, are you?"

Actually, I thought to myself, *there's another game on after this.* Unmet expectations are not limited to Saturday afternoons, but extend to birthday-celebration protocol. My first birthday celebration as a married man got off to a rocky start. Noreen let me sleep in, and I awoke to a silent house. I walk into our kitchen and was slightly, yet undeniably, disappointed. No birthday card was waiting for me on the kitchen counter or dining-room table. My parents always, *always* had a card waiting first thing on a birthday morning. *Maybe,* I thought, *Noreen forgot and is now out buying a card.* At the time, I didn't know what a communication climate was, but I could feel our climate start to get frosty. I'd later learn that in Noreen's family, the birthday card was presented after dinner with cake and gifts.

Here's the point: if you had asked me before I got married if I had an expectation about Saturday afternoons or birthday cards, I would have laughed. Having an expectation about the time of day when a card should be given would have seemed ridiculous.

One way Noreen and I have found it helpful to address expectations is to create an evolving list of them. Our list answers questions like these:

- Who cleans up after dinner?
- Who makes dinner?
- How often do we want the TV on?
- Who should plan/lead family devotionals?
- Who's responsible for getting kids started on homework?
- What are expectations for Saturday afternoon (relax or home projects)?
- What makes date night a date night (talking over coffee or playing tennis)?

- Who plans anniversary celebrations?
- How many times a week do we as a family want to eat together?

Your list will look different, and it will evolve as situations come up and as expectations arise that you didn't even know you had. The expectations Noreen had for me when we were twentysomethings without kids were very different from those she had when we thirtysomethings with three young boys (two in diapers). Revising and updating an expectations list requires a continual flow of open and honest communication. Being open about expectations can be surprisingly difficult.

Unspoken expectations. One of the key findings of the researchers at Heroit-Watt University in Edinburgh was that romantic comedies plant in us an idea that our soul mate ought to anticipate our deepest needs without our having to voice them. In other words, our spouse ought to know in certain situations what is important to us; we shouldn't have to spell it out. Such an idea, whether fostered by romantic blockbusters or not, is disastrous to a communication climate.

A few years back, Noreen gave me an anniversary card that I've shared with audiences every time I've spoken on this issue of expectations, because it perfectly illustrates what I'm describing.

I'll never forget that day. When I got home from work, Noreen gave me the card. The front read, "Honey, Here's what I'm hoping for on our anniversary! HOT SEX NOW!"

Well, you can imagine how happy I was to receive such a card expressing this unspoken expectation. Earlier that week, I had made reservations for dinner at a local restaurant known for its romantic atmosphere. During all my planning, I had the expectation that the evening would end precisely in the manner described on the card. Then I opened the card.

Holding hands	Openly talking	Watching BalleT
Sharing dreams	Enjoying time together	Time to RelaX
Nice long walk	Out to dinner	Recall hoW (we met)

When I share this card with audiences, I still laugh. My unspoken expectations focused on the capitals, while Noreen's focused on the expanded version. Both of them are so obvious to each of us that we are sure the other will get it. Of *course* celebrating an anniversary will include holding hands, recalling how we met, going out to dinner, sharing dreams, enjoying time together and sex. Right? The problem with unspoken expectations is what happens to the communication climate when the unthinkable happens—the expectation isn't met. So, when it comes to expectations, the general rule is this: let your spouse know what you are hoping will happen in a situation *in advance*.

If the organizers of the Twenty-Ninth Olympic Games would have taken the attitude that you can't do anything about the weather, two billon viewers worldwide might have missed a dazzling opening-night production due to severe rain showers. With ominous clouds on the horizon, they developed a plan and took action. Through time and consistent effort, communication climates, like the skies over the National Stadium, can change. However, you may have noticed that in our discussion of how to improve communication climates we have yet to address the issue of trust. Communication experts agree that the level of trust that exists between spouses is foundational to the health of a marriage and thus warrants it own chapter.

THINK IT OVER

1. To acknowledge your spouse, catch her doing what's right. Make a list of five things your spouse has done right in the last few days, and share it with her.

2. What's your sacred history? Write down the following: when you first met, your first kiss, getting engaged, your wedding day, buying your first house, celebrating your first anniversary, birth of children (if applicable), first Christmas together and so on. Remember, all of these investments would be lost if your marriage ended.

3. Are you a community of two or members of a broader community? How would belonging to a broader community (church, extended family, neighborhood) help lessen the emotional or relational needs you place on your spouse? What steps can you take to become more rooted in a community outside your marriage?

4. What is the list of evolving expectations that, if not addressed, could put a strain on your marital climate? Each of you, make a list of expectations separately, and then share them with each other.

Strengthening Trust
in Your Climate

*I*n the movie *Fireproof*, Kirk Cameron plays a firefighter named Caleb who has lost the trust and love of his wife through his addiction to pornography and frequent bursts of anger. Their communication climate is so toxic, they can hardly stand to be in the same room. Out of desperation, he accepts his father's advice to try to win his wife back by doing something positive for her every day for forty days.

The first day, though Caleb doesn't feel like doing it, he pours her a cup of coffee as she heads off to work. She glances at it and mumbles, "Not thirsty," as she leaves. The next day he vacuums the living room; she notices, but no response. This goes on day after day. On day fifteen, after deep soul-searching, Caleb destroys the computer he had watched porn on and replaces it with a rose and a carefully handwritten note: "I choose you!" No reaction from her. Why?

In the previous chapter, we said that through careful planning and consistent effort, communication climates can change. Why, then, haven't the efforts of this firefighter made any positive impact on the climate of his troubled marriage? Part of the answer comes from the observations of Mahatma Gandhi: "The moment there is suspicion about a person's motives, everything he does becomes tainted."[1] Early in *Fireproof* we learn that the wife is suspicious of her husband's actions because she thinks the only reason he's pouring her coffee, cleaning and giving up porn is to soften her up for the divorce when they'll have to negotiate who gets what in terms of their possessions. In short, he's simply softening her up for the kill.

While trust is merely one element of a communication climate, it warrants its own chapter because it is the *foundational* issue of every couple's communication climate. Without trust being firmly established, nothing else can proceed. If you don't trust your spouse's intentions, every attempt he or she makes to apply the principles of this book will be met with a suspicious response: "What's he doing?" "She never sits next to me on the couch; I wonder if she needs something done around the house." "He just gave me hug while I was doing dishes; I wonder if he expects we'll be intimate after the kids go to bed."

ESTABLISHING TRUST

There are two types of trust: self-trust and relational trust. Self-trust focuses on the trustworthiness of an individual, while relational trust is the trust that exists between two people.

Self-trust. Nearly all of us want others to think of us as good, honest and trustworthy people. But are we? The Greek philosopher Plato had a test to measure a person's virtue and trustworthiness. He would say to audiences, "Imagine I gave you a ring that, when you put it on, made you invisible to human sight. In what situations would you choose to wear it?"[2] For Plato, the test would be to see if a person's words matched her actions. For example, you could tell your wife that you have strong convictions against watching movies that contain sexual content; yet

simply slip on the ring, and you can go see *any* movie unde-
tected. Or tell your spouse that you completely trust him in
how he talks about you to his friends when they come to shoot
pool downstairs, and what's the harm in slipping on the ring
and going downstairs to eavesdrop, just to be *sure*. For Plato,
virtue (integrity, trustworthiness, honor) is not who you are
when people are watching; it is who you are even when no one
is present.

The first step in establishing trust in your marital climate
has nothing to do with your relationship with your spouse. It is
to ask the question "Am I trustworthy as a person?" Like King
David, we need to ask of the Lord regularly: "Search me, O
God, and know my heart; test me and know my anxious
thoughts. See if there is any offensive way in me" (Psalm 139:23-
24).

Asking the Lord to search your heart is not for the faint of
heart. This week, find a quiet place and ask God the following
concerning your self-trust:

• Do I usually tell the truth to my spouse, or half-truths?

• Are there areas about which I find it difficult to tell my
  spouse the truth?

• Am I trustworthy when it comes to issues of sexual temptation?

• Am I trustworthy when it comes to financial stewardship?

• Am I a person of my word? Do I usually follow through on
  what I say I'm going to do?

• Do I live out the values in private that I talk about in public?

• If I possessed Plato's ring, how would I use it?

As you go through these questions and a time of introspec-
tion, it is important to remember that if you are a follower of
Christ, there is no condemnation (see Romans 8:1) if you real-

ize that you often fall short of God's or your own standards. However, Christ does want you to live a life of integrity in which your actions match your profession of faith. If the climate is healthy between you and your spouse, consider sharing some of these answers with her or him so that this is not an exercise only between you and God.

Relational trust. Relationship expert Julia Wood writes that relational trust has two dimensions. First, it entails confidence that others are reliable. "We count on them to do what they say and not to do what they promise they won't."[3] Many of us can think of a small group of friends and family that we can, in a pinch, count on. My wife's best friend is her older sister, Kathleen, who has always been there for her and us. When tough times hit our family, it's Kathleen who says, "Tell me you need me, and I'm there tomorrow on the next flight. Count on it." In graphic language, the writer of Proverbs describes what it is like to rely on a person who *doesn't* reward your trust: "Like a bad tooth or a lame foot is reliance on the unfaithful in times of trouble" (25:19). While our spouses aren't perfect, and factors can happen outside their control, we trust that they have every intention of being there for us when we need them.

Second, relational trust assumes that our spouse cares about our personal welfare. We expect our spouse to look out for us and not to look for opportunities to hurt us. We trust that our spouse is happy for our successes and sad for us when we fail. Because we trust that our spouse loves us, it doesn't occur to us that he would lie to us, because a "lying tongue hates those it hurts" (Proverbs 26:28).

But what if those close to us don't look out for our well-being? Some of us have histories that negatively influence our ability to trust others or our spouse. In chapter one I suggested it's helpful at times to ask who's in the room with you. If your parents were consistent in following through on their promises and commitments, you most likely find it easy to trust others. However, if your primary caregiver was inconsistent in keeping commitments, and trust was often broken, your capacity to trust others was, to varying degrees, compromised. Researchers believe that those formative years with our parents or primary caregivers creates an attachment style that teaches us how to approach relationships. For example, a fearful attachment style is created when parents communicate in consistently negative, or even abusive, ways and frequently undermine the trust you placed in them as a child. Thus, children learn to see themselves as unlovable and others as unworthy of trust.[4]

Relational trust does not develop overnight, but in a gradual process that takes time and grows in degrees. Wood notes that we "learn to trust people over time as we interact with them and discover they do what they say they will and they don't betray us."[5] But what happens when people don't do what they say? What happens when people betray our trust?

As a nation, we received a powerful example of what broken trust looks like in the media frenzy that surrounded the marital struggles of John and Elizabeth Edwards. During the 2008 presidential campaign, John had an affair with former campaign worker Rielle Hunter and fathered a child with her. He initially denied the affair but later admitted it, while disputing the paternity of the child.

After enduring public humiliation and while still processing the pain, Elizabeth Edwards granted an interview in 2009 with Larry King. In it she described John coming to her after the story broke and confessing the affair. In no uncertain terms, he had told her that it was a single occurrence of poor judgment.

My wife and I watched this interview, and I will never forget what we witnessed next. With deep pain still etched in her eyes, she told King that John had lied to her. It had not been a single indiscretion. The affair had been ongoing. "How did you feel about that?" asked King. "It was pretty devastating," she responded, averting her eyes from the camera. Even though she had forgiven him, "the work on rebuilding trust was set back a great deal. . . . We're still working on that."[6] Initially John had claimed the child wasn't his, but in 2010 the truth came out, and he confirmed paternity. Elizabeth was heartbroken, and John moved out.

What can we learn about rebuilding trust from this tragic situation? First, in defining truthfulness, Jesus simply tells his followers that they should let their "yes be yes" and their "no be no" (see Matthew 5:37). In a world of political spin and carefully calculated half-truths, Jesus tells his followers to tell the truth. Rebuilding trust with a person means that she or he deserves the right to hear the full truth from us, no matter how awkward or painful that may be for us in telling it. If you have broken a trust with your spouse, you need to come clean with her. John Edwards compounded the problem by lying about the extent of the affair and the identity of the child. Though it would have been initially more hurtful to Elizabeth, he needed to tell her the entire truth up front.

Second, the person who breaks the trust needs to realize that just as trust is built gradually, it is also rebuilt gradually. After having caught one of my boys in a lie, I showed him through an object lesson how his lie had depleted my trust. I blew up a large balloon and handed it to him without tying the end in a knot and told him to hold it. "Do you know what this is?" I asked. "A balloon?" he responded sheepishly. "No. It's my trust in you." I then told him to let go of it. We both watched as it flew across the room and eventually fell to the ground. I told him that just as the balloon would have to be refilled again breath by breath, my trust in him would also have to be rebuilt. If you've lost the trust of your spouse, you'll need to earn it back.

Each time you use the credit card responsibly, trust is slowly restored.

Each time the history on your computer shows no porn sites visited, trust increases.

Each time verbal abuse is replaced with restraint, trust grows.

Each time a promise is kept, trust is fostered and the communication climate becomes more and more positive.

I wish this idea of earning back trust applied only to high-profile politicians or teenage sons who are occasionally less than truthful. One morning my wife let me sleep late. I eventually woke up to the smell of hot coffee as Noreen walked in with a breakfast tray complete with a rose, the morning sports page and a card. As she walked away, she said, "How do you want your eggs?" "Hey, what's all this?" I exclaimed as she went, wiping the sleep from my eyes. *I have the most romantic, spontaneous wife,* I thought to myself. *People say marriage is work. What's work about this?*

I picked up the card—which she had kissed with cherry-red lipstick—opened it, and read, "HAPPY ANNIVERSARY!" What? I slowly, horrifyingly, looked at the date on my watch. Yep. May 12. *"Hey, what's all this?"* Did I really say that?

Dead silence from the kitchen. Yeah, I said it.

In every marriage, there are two sets of rules. *Explicit rules* are openly discussed by spouses. *Implicit rules* are assumed by both and are discussed only if violated. One of the implicit rules of our marriage is that we take time to thoughtfully celebrate our anniversaries *and* that the husband takes the lead in planning that celebration. While we never discussed that it was my responsibility to remember and plan a celebration, Noreen trusted me to make the celebration of our anniversary a priority.

She was right to trust me. Early in our courtship and marriage, I had earned her trust that I would be attentive to special events like birthdays and anniversaries. Once earned, I had maintained her trust through surprise parties, gifts, poems and so on. I had to recognize that by completely forgetting our anniversary I hurt her. I had to also admit that I had failed to live up to my own standards of being an attentive husband (loss of self-trust). Once I realized what had happened, I went to Noreen and apologized. However, as with my son, I needed to realize that Noreen's trust in me and my credibility had to be reestablished.

The word *credibility* comes from the Latin root *credere*, meaning "to believe." I've taken some steps to help Noreen believe in me again when it comes to anniversaries. First, I've not missed an anniversary since. How detrimental would it be to our communication climate if I apologized to Noreen for forgetting our anniversary but then forgot it the very next year? The Scriptures make a clear distinction between lament (showing remorse for a wrongdoing) and repentance (changing the action). Lament without repentance makes a mockery of attempts to rebuild trust. Second, I've taken small, concrete steps to ensure success. For example, every year before school starts, I purchase a new personal calendar. The first thing I do, even before I put my name and phone number in the front, is to write down our anniversary and the birthdays of Noreen and the boys. I've even started writing myself a note one month before our anniversary so it doesn't catch me by surprise and I have time to plan.

Protecting Trust

While there are many reasons to protect the trust that exists between you and your spouse, let me offer one that particularly motivates me: the pain that breaking trust causes my wife. Correctional institutions have been experimenting with a promising new treatment in changing the behavior of violent offenders. In one program, offenders read stories of victims of the specific crimes they have committed. Rapists read the narratives of rape victims, muggers read the stories of assault victims, and drunken drivers become aware of the devastating impact of their actions on others. By reading these firsthand accounts and even seeing video testimonies of victims, perpetrators see, hear and witness the pain their actions have caused. Many graduates of the program report that they never forget the faces or narratives they have been exposed to and have successfully altered their lifestyles.[7]

If John Edwards could have seen in advance the pain on his wife's face when they discussed his infidelity, would he still have gone through with it? If he'd known that she'd use the word *devastating* to describe the pain his actions had caused, would he so easily have ruptured his wife's trust? Anticipating the effects of our actions is the strategy the Scriptures incorporate when James asks his readers to consider how their words can cause damage to others. He has them imagine standing in the middle of a forest that has been torched to blackened ash by the spark of one little flame (see 3:5). He forcefully tells his readers that the tongue is also a flame that torches a person's body and life (see v. 6).

What motivates me to keep Noreen's trust is to imagine the pain in her eyes and the devastation that would surely result if that trust were to be broken. And what of my three boys? If I broke their trust in me to be faithful to their mother and to them, would I hinder their capacity to trust their future spouses later in life? Not only would my marriage suffer, but their future marriages would as well.

THINK IT OVER

1. Gandhi stated, "The moment there is suspicion about a person's motives, everything he does becomes tainted." Do you

agree? Why is a lack of trust in a person's motives so potentially devastating to a relationship?

2. If you were given Plato's ring, how would you be tempted to use it? Are you often good only because you fear being caught for doing wrong?

3. Concerning self-trust, how would you answer these questions:

   • Do I usually tell the truth to my spouse, or half-truths?

   • Are there areas where I find it difficult to tell my spouse the truth?

   • Am I trustworthy when it comes to issues of sexual temptation?

   • Am I trustworthy when it comes to financial stewardship?

   • Am I a person of my word? Do I usually follow through on what I say I'm going to do?

   • Do I live out the values in private that I talk about in public?

Talking Your Way into a
Supportive Climate

*H*ave you ever played Whack-a-Mole?

It's an arcade game where you stand at a waist-level cabinet holding a rubber mallet. On the surface of the cabinet are five holes. Randomly, up from a hole pops an electronic mole, and your job is to hit it as soon as it rears its head. The more quickly you whack it, the more points you get.

Noreen has commented that many couples have a communication pattern that resembles Whack-a-Mole. One partner says something, and the other is waiting with a verbal club to pounce. Every idea or suggestion is met with an air of superiority accompanied by a verbal whack. "Honey, don't you think we should first . . ." Whack! "Hey, what would you think if we . . ." Whack! Whack! "I know you said we didn't have the money for this, but I thought . . ." Whack! Whack! *Whack!* Eventually, the spouse gives up. In the arcade game, if you keep putting in quarters, the moles will keep popping up to get a beating. In a communication climate with our spouse, we may stop offering our opinion altogether if we feel it would be demeaned.

Communication scholar Jack Gibb, after years of watching individuals interact, began to notice positive and negative patterns in communication climates. Specifically, he identified six forms of communication that move individuals toward a defensive climate and six that produce a more supportive climate.[1] Do we communicate in a manner that promotes a positive climate or one that compares to Whack-a-Mole? In the following pages we'll look at differing styles of communication in the form of six pairings that offer us choices—choices that make all the difference in the type of climate we experience.

STRATEGY VERSUS SPONTANEITY

A few years ago, I participated in a debate with a former evangelist turned atheist. My opponent had a degree in religion, had written numerous books attacking the Christian faith and had belonged to a high-IQ society that required members to be in the 99.997th percentile. In front of a packed auditorium on the campus of Marshall University in Huntington, West Virginia, we debated whether Jesus' resurrection was fact or fantasy. It's the oddest feeling knowing that while you are speaking another person is listening to every word, looking for contradictions, inconsistencies and other weaknesses. Even when he asked a seemingly innocent question, I felt he had a secret agenda and that I was playing into his hands. I left the debate drained. To have to weigh *every* word you say is mentally and emotionally exhausting.

This is what Gibb means by a strategy approach to communication. During a conversation with your spouse, do you sometimes feel that you are participating in a mental chess match? Your spouse asks, "Do you have plans Saturday morning?" When you answer no, he or she pounces: "Then there's no reason you can't help me clean the garage." Checkmate. These types of questions are referred to as *counterfeit questions* that are strategically designed to trap a person. The result is that in future conversations you become increasingly defensive and protective in your answers.

In contrast, spontaneous communication is free of manipulation. Spontaneity does not mean that you say whatever you are thinking during a conversation, nor does it mean that you can't choose to be silent and carefully process your answer before articulating it. Being spontaneous *primarily* means that you feel the freedom to offer opinions that are still in process, without the fear that any inconsistencies or contradictions you utter will be immediately attacked.

My wife and I regularly meet with a group of four couples to discuss everything from marriage to theology to movies to the Super Bowl. Conversations often start with, "I haven't fully thought this out, but what if . . . " While good-natured ribbing is part of our conversations, there is freedom to offer an opinion that's still in process. At the center of a spontaneous approach to communication is *trust*. I trust you not to use my words against me as I openly work out my response to important issues. I also trust that the questions you ask (such as "Do you have plans for Saturday morning?") are not presented with a secret agenda.

NEUTRALITY VERSUS EMPATHY

When speaking with a person, we can become defensive if we perceive our thoughts, passions and convictions are met with detached, distant neutrality. Whenever I think of Gibb's idea of detached neutrality, I remember being stranded in a Memphis airport. My wife and I had been flying all day with three exhausted boys. All we wanted to do was get on this last flight and head home. When I went to pick up our boarding passes, I was informed that my entire family had been bumped from the flight. "Sir, we are in an oversold situation and needed to place your family on a later flight," the agent said in a matter-of-fact way. I explained we'd been flying all day and the kids were worn out. Without looking up, she responded, "Sir, on the back of your ticket, it's written that we reserve the right to bump individuals at our discretion." Her voice was cool, controlled and uninterested. Mine was not. I *again* explained our situation. She looked over my shoulder at the line forming and said, "Next." As I walked away to plot my next move, I was frustrated beyond words. How could she not even acknowledge the tiredness of my family?

Imagine getting that kind of response from a spouse. Two weeks after being stranded in the airport, I was speaking with a couple at a marriage workshop, and she was telling me how her husband's desire to finish graduate school—while working two jobs—was killing the family. "I never see him anymore," she said. "I'm starting to believe that a degree is more important than me and the kids." As she spoke, powerful emotions started to surface.

And I'll never forget his response. With not a trace of emotion, he replied, "I've been gone a lot." That was it. I waited for him to say more, but he didn't. In five lifeless words, he summarized her pain and concern. The tone of his voice matched that of the disinterested flight agent. Marriage expert John Gottman states that regularly distancing yourself from your spouse emotionally and psychologically—which he calls *stonewalling*—is *the* most destructive habit you can form in a marriage.

The opposite of neutrality is empathy. The word *empathy* originates from two Greek words that together mean "feeling inside." Based on this definition, empathy is the attempt to experience and acknowledge the emotions of another. The call to empathy is vividly expressed by the writer of Hebrews, who encourages us to empathize with persecuted Christians. We are called not only to "remember those in prison" who are mistreated, but to do so "as if you yourselves were suffering" (13:3). We are directed to imagine prison life, and all the emotions associated with it, through the perspective of those imprisoned. If the Memphis ticket agent had said, "Mr. Muehlhoff, I can imagine how frustrating this must be for you. You and your family have had a long day and now we've made it longer. I'd be upset as well," that would have been much better. What if the husband in my workshop had said to his discouraged wife, "Trying to pick up the slack at home while I juggle work and school must be exhausting. I know I've not been around much, and that must be difficult for you and the kids." Empathy does not mean that you completely agree with a person's assessment; it means that you attempt to see life through the perspective of your spouse. Author Maria Lugones creatively calls empathy "world-traveling"; you leave your familiar surroundings and enter into the social and personal world of another.

CERTAINTY VERSUS PROVISIONALISM

Have you run into individuals who are certain they are right concerning an issue? Individuals whose words are laced with dogmatism and who are absolutely certain they have a corner on the truth and seek to demean anyone who disagrees? "I'm telling you right now, that'll never work." "That's not how I would do it." "I can't see you going anywhere in that profession." "I'd never let my kids get involved in that." "Clearly, the Bible teaches that we should believe this." If you've ever had those phrases directed at you, you understand why certainty language fosters defensiveness and shuts down communication.

The frustration caused by a person deadlocked in her or his position was vividly described by jurors in the corruption trial of a former sheriff in the county where I live. After the verdict, juror after juror said the sheriff was acquitted on most of the criminal counts—though they thought he was guilty—because one juror, referred to as Jim, started the deliberations by sitting in a chair, putting his hands behind his head and saying, "Not guilty, didn't do it." The forcefulness in his voice and defensive posture established a negative climate in the room. Jurors agreed that his refusal to even consider the arguments of others was the "kiss of death" for any meaningful deliberations. (Interestingly, the paper reported that Jim's full-time job was working as the Mad Hatter at Disneyland.)

I can't be too hard on Jim, because I've done the same thing in my marriage with the same results. After deciding what to do concerning an issue, I confidently pronounce my decision to Noreen. The message my wife receives is clear: I know what I'm doing, and nothing you can say will change my mind. Case closed. Conversation ended.

While certainty language discourages alternative views, provisionalism welcomes such views by expressing a willingness to reconsider long-held positions and convictions. I was first introduced to this way of thinking in a philosophy class. The professor started the class by having us write down our strongest convictions. In no time, I filled three pages of a legal notepad. While we wrote, the professor put a quote on the board: "In all matters, it is profitable to place a question mark over things long believed to be true." He wasn't saying that we should not have convictions about important issues. He was simply saying that we need to revisit our views occasionally to gain additional information. It's an attitude that changes how we think *and* talk about issues.

Julia Wood writes, "Provisional communication includes statements such as, 'The way I see the issue is . . . ' 'One way to look at this is . . . ' and 'Probably what I would do in that situation is . . . '"[2] Such phrases communicate to our spouse that our view of an issue or position is not the only way to approach it. Benjamin Franklin, one of our most astute political minds, wrote that before he spoke about anything, even his most passionate beliefs, he would insert one word: *perhaps*. The Scriptures forcefully state that "God opposes the proud but gives grace to the humble" (1 Peter 5:5). A communication climate is made more affirming not by spouses abandoning convictions about marriage or family but by them being open to the views of others.

SUPERIORITY VERSUS EQUALITY

Most of us feel more comfortable when interacting with others who treat us as if we are equal instead of inferior. The climate quickly becomes defensive when we encounter others who project an attitude of superiority. This inferiority is acutely felt by the interns and patients of Dr. Gregory House, the main character in the hit show *House*. House is rude, sarcastic and brilliant. His powers of observation make him the leading expert in diagnostic medicine. The problem is, he knows it. House believes his ideas are vastly superior to those of medical journals, other experts and even million-dollar machines. If the results of an MRI or CAT scan fail to support his diagnosis, the machine must be malfunctioning. As you can expect, House has no friends. Who would want to spend time around a person who continually makes you feel inferior?

Unfortunately, I think all of us have a little House residing in us when it comes to certain issues. I know I do. I've taught and written about communication for more than twenty years. The focus of my Ph.D. was marital communication and how couples can resolve differences. When Noreen and I find ourselves embroiled in a disagreement, I often feel a little House welling up. The tone of my voice changes as I, the expert, pronounce how we should resolve our differences. Understandably, my I-know-more-about-this-than-you-do attitude puts Noreen on the defensive and strains the conversation.

In contrast to Gregory House, I have a friend who models what it means to treat others as equals. This friend is a world-class philosopher who has written more than thirty books. Yet every time we are together, he not only welcomes my ideas, but seeks them out. He never makes me feel that his ideas are vastly superior to mine. "We can have exceptional experience or ability in certain areas and still show regard for others and their contribution to interaction," Wood writes.[3] While my friend knows more about philosophy than I do, he still shows a high regard for my opinions. The same can be true in marriage. In every marriage, one spouse will no doubt have more knowledge or expertise in an area than the other. The issue isn't who knows more, but that both partners feel valued while interacting.

EVALUATION VERSUS DESCRIPTION

When people engage in evaluation, they judge the actions and motives of another. The tell-tale sign of an evaluator is the use of *you*. "You are not committed to this relationship!" "You care about your job more than me." "You are self-centered." "You'd rather go hang out with your friends than spend time with me." Evaluators are convinced that they have insight into the whys behind a person's actions. A husband is late for dinner; he doesn't care about family time. A wife goes to bed early; she's not interested in sexual intimacy. Kids start playing video games before doing homework; they are intentionally breaking family rules.

In contrast, descriptive language comments on the actions of a person without passing judgment or claiming to know the motive behind the action. How we comment on the actions of our spouse can have a significant impact on our communication climate. One of the odd habits I have from growing up in an old house in East Detroit that had no dishwasher is that, without thinking, I put dirty dishes in the sink, even though the dishwasher is empty. It's frustrating for Noreen to find dishes in the sink when the dishwasher is two feet away. How she brings it up has a powerful impact on our climate. "Are you too lazy to put your dishes away?" will surely cause a chill, while "I've noticed you put a dish in the sink when the dishwasher is empty" is much easier to receive.

CONTROLLING VERSUS PROBLEM ORIENTATION

Every couple experiences a difference of opinion once in a while. "Can we afford to go on vacation this year?" "Should we homeschool?" "Is it wise to spend all that money on a TV?" "Will we let our kids be on sports teams that require missing church on Sunday?" "How much debt is too much?" "Is it time to start a family?" Controlling communicators know exactly how to answer these questions and attempt to manipulate the conversation and force their perspective on others. Problem-oriented communicators seek, as much as possible, to discover solutions that are beneficial and equitable to everyone.

Having three boys who all play sports can create a hectic schedule and feed into a strong sense of hurrysickness. Noreen and I once figured out that if we went to every one of our boy's baseball games, we'd spend 150 hours sitting in the stands— *not* including playoffs. A disagreement arose between us concerning eating meals together as a family after games. Noreen valued carving out time to eat a home-cooked meal, while I'd rather zip in and out of drive-through so we could rest or do school work when we got home. Noreen viewed sitting down at the dinner table as a time of connection; I viewed the preparation and cleanup as more work. Simply put, we were at an impasse. Invoking a controlling orientation would mean both of us trying to manipulate the other into adopting a preferred solution. A problem-oriented approach would entail us creating a solution that respects and incorporates the values of each person. Paul regularly exhorts believers to look "not only to your own interests, but also to the interests of others" (Philippians 2:4). We finally decided that once during the week and once on the weekend, we'd shoot to have a sit-down meal and reconnect as a family.

After years of studying couples, Gibb noticed an immense difference between couples who tended to experience supportive climates and those that had defensive ones. But before looking at his conclusion, a word should be said about the six forms of communication we've just considered. For us to see how defensive and supportive climates are formed, Gibb purposely framed these options as stark contrasts or opposite ends of a spectrum, such as superiority versus equality, certainty versus provisionalism and neutrality versus empathy. He fully understood that there are times when neutrality needs to be exhibited over empathy, such as when a doctor chooses to remain somewhat emotionally detached while telling a patient she has cancer. However, the neutrality Gibb describes is that of a doctor who is so detached he doesn't even acknowledge—verbally or nonverbally—the distraught person in front of him. The same could be said about certainty language. All of us have the right to speak with conviction to our spouse concerning key issues in the marriage.

For Gibb, certainty language demeans a person and slams the door on all other views. What Gibb tries to help us recognize is what communication scholars have long believed: all communication exists on two levels. The *content level* expresses the literal or denotative meaning of the words being spoken. The *relationship level* expresses the amount of liking, responsiveness, respect and power that exists between two people. For Gibb, how you speak your convictions—with certainty or provisionalism—will determine the type of relational climate you and your spouse experience. The same principle is seen when Paul commands us to speak "the truth [content] in love [relationship]" (Ephesians 4:15). To demean your spouse with certainty language, regardless of the context or truth of what you are saying, is to foster a defensive climate.

Gibb's final conclusion was that couples who regularly engage in extreme forms of evaluation, neutrality, strategy, controlling orientation, certainty and superiority experience a defensive climate, while those utilizing description, empathy, spontaneity, problem orientation, provisionalism and equality create a positive climate. These important decisions in how we communicate set the tone in our marriage and the intimacy we experience. As an executive consultant who helps corporate leaders communicate more effectively, Susan Scott, notes, "Relationships exist in the conversations that make them up."[4]

The last three chapters have given you a strategy to strengthen the overall climate of your marriage. But what if your spouse decides she or he isn't interested in strengthening the climate? What if there comes a season in the marriage when you find yourself acting alone in trying to improve the climate? If or when that time comes, you have two options.

First, you can respond in kind, and allow the climate to continue to deteriorate. Your spouse doesn't invest in the relationship, so you stop investing as well. Your spouse doesn't make an effort to acknowledge you, so you refuse to acknowledge him or her, and so on. Communication scholars call this a negative spiral: the actions of one person accelerate the actions of the other person. Both negative and positive spirals "tend to pick up momentum that feeds back on itself—closeness and harmony builds more closeness and harmony; misunderstanding and dissatisfaction creates more misunderstanding and dissatisfaction," states conflict management expert William Wilmot.[5] Wilmot concludes: "Usually, one person thinks the other has 'begun' the conflict, and that he/she is simply an innocent party responding to unreasonable behavior. This leads to conflict that spirals out of control."[6] When your spouse decides, for whatever reason, not to work on the climate of your marriage, your first inclination may be to stop working also. Be warned—such a decision may result in a climate that spirals toward apathy, bitterness and even dissolution. For those of us interested in cultivating marriages that honor God, this option is not an option at all.

Your other option is to continue working on the climate, whether or not your spouse participates. While such an option is wildly counterintuitive, it has three benefits. First, your unconditional investment in the climate keeps a negative spiral from gaining momentum. If both spouses stop attending to the health of a relationship, the spiral will pick up momentum, isolation quickly breeds more isolation, and selfishness breeds more selfishness. Wilmot suggests that the surest way to keep a negative spiral in check is to "alter your usual response—do what comes unnaturally."[7] In other words, resist the natural urge to match your spouse's apathy toward the relationship, and instead be attentive to the climate.

Second, your effort will lay the groundwork for the start of a positive spiral between you and your spouse. I once knew a husband who became consumed with graduate school. After work, every minute of his free time was spent studying. While feeling hurt and neglected, his wife made the decision to continue to invest in their climate. Almost a year into his program, he unexpectedly called her to have lunch. During this short lunch, he didn't apologize or even comment on his misguided priorities. When it was over, she acknowledged their pleasant conversation and his invitation. She had hoped for much, much more, but decided simply to affirm him. A month later, he set up another short lunch. Slowly, a positive spiral started to develop. In the next few months, they had many more lunches, and their climate got to the point where they could discuss his overcommitted scheduled. If she had not consistently and selflessly worked on the climate, the positive spiral would never have developed.

Third, spouses who commit unconditionally to the health of their marital climate often experience God's love in profound ways. In his insightful book *How to Save Your Marriage Alone*, Ed Wheat makes this comment: "When you choose the pathway of irrevocable commitment to your mate and your marriage . . . you will find that choice leading you into a place of *agape* love and peace and personal growth."[8]

The word *agape* is the most common word for love in the New Testament. It refers to self-giving love that flows toward a person who is utterly unworthy. One of the defining features of *agape* love is that "it is given quite irrespective of merit, and it is a love that seeks to give."[9] While we were still sinners, God pursued us and sacrificed Christ (see Romans 5:8). When we choose to love our spouse by unconditionally investing in our climates—regardless of what we perceive our spouse's merit to be—we come to understand God's *agape* love toward us. A spouse seeking to love his or her nonresponsive spouse with *agape* love must seek out daily encouragement, according to Wheat. "It is important to fill your mind with positive biblical input: biblical counseling, preaching, and teaching; good books and Bible-study tapes; and friends who will affirm you in your commitment to your marriage."[10]

THINK IT OVER

1. As you look at your overall climate, how many of the positive traits presented by Gibb apply, as opposed to defensive traits?

2. To develop your skill at supportive communication, translate

the following statements from evaluative to descriptive:

Evaluative: You care more about work than about your family.

Descriptive:

Evaluative: Obviously, being on time doesn't matter to you.

Descriptive:

Evaluative: You always let the house get so messy.

Descriptive:

3. When it comes to *superiority*, in what areas (finances, parenting, in-laws, church) is it easy for you to adopt a Dr. Gregory House attitude toward your spouse? How could you approach that same issue with more equality, as described by Gibb?

4. Maria Lugones describes empathy as traveling into the world of another and experiencing life from her or his perspective. What is one area in which you wish your spouse would enter your world and attempt to see it from your point of view?

5. Why is it so difficult to work on your marital climate when you feel your spouse isn't doing his or her share? How does being a recipient of God's *agape* love—unmerited love toward you—help you extend *agape* love toward your spouse?

Taking a Reading of
Your Marriage

*H*ow do I know when the time is right to bring up an issue with my husband?"

So began a long, strongly worded email written to me after I spoke at a marriage retreat. The woman had been married for two years to a man fresh out of law school who was one year into a demanding job at a law firm. They had a baby in diapers, cash was tight, stress was high, and there never seemed to be a good time to talk. As a result, key issues between them were being put on the back burner, and tension was starting to rise. In short, she wrote, they needed to talk. But when? She wrote that when she tried to bring up issues, he seemed distracted and increasingly defensive, which caused her to back off. The last thing she wanted was to nag him or make him angry. She concluded it was easier for them just to sit and watch TV.

I first explained what a communication climate is and encouraged her to intentionally cultivate a positive climate with her husband. I recommended she hold off bringing up issues to her husband until she felt the climate was strong enough to have a productive conversation. It is the word spoken in the right circumstance that the writers of Proverbs compare to fine jewelry (see 25:11). How a person knows the circumstance is right brings us to the opening question of her email.

The second part of my answer to this perplexed woman is the focus of this chapter: *How can we learn to take a climate reading of our marriage in order to maximize communication with our spouse?* A crucial part of strengthening a climate is learning to ascertain to what degree your efforts have worked and if the moment is right to initiate a conversation with your spouse. Preparation is only half of the equation.

Knowing if the timing is right played a crucial role in one of the greatest events of World War II. On June 6, 1944, more than 130,000 American and British soldiers waited for the go-ahead to storm the beaches of Normandy. For an entire year, the Allied invasion had been meticulously planned. Coordinating air attacks, naval fire support, and the transportation of soldiers and machines had been a logistical nightmare. All that was needed was the approval of one man you've probably never heard of: J. M. Stagg. Stagg was not a general or a military strategist. He was, however, Dwight Eisenhower's chief meteorologist. Eisenhower and the entire Allied force looked to him to pick the day that would have the best weather to ensure success. Conditions didn't need to be perfect, but they did need to be suitable for the largest amphibious invasion in history. After a sleepless night, Stagg gave the okay, and D-Day became history.

What we can learn from Stagg and the events surrounding Normandy *isn't* that we should wait for the right circumstances to pounce on our spouse to get the upper hand. Rather, it's that we should learn to read the climate of our marriage to know when it's conducive to having a productive, give-and-take conversation. Remember, the conditions don't need to be perfect to have a productive conversation. You simply want the climate to work with you, not against you. Learning to read the current climate of your marriage is crucial for planning future interaction.

HOW TO TAKE A READING OF YOUR MARRIAGE

There are three aspects to taking a read of your marital climate. First, determine how you feel about the climate. Second, imagine how your spouse feels. Third, check your perceptions with your spouse. Below you'll find a series of questions exploring each of the aspects of a marital climate. Notice that these questions ask you to first assign a number value (one being the lowest and five being the highest) and then ask a follow-up question that allows you to write down thoughts and dig a little deeper. For some people, numbers help clarify their thinking, while for others, being able to write out complete sentences furthers the evaluation process. Remember, first you answer these questions. When finished, go back and answer how you think your spouse would respond to these questions. Then go and talk it over with your spouse.

If these questions start to feel daunting, remember that there are always two ways to check the weather. If you want to quickly gauge the weather, pop your head out the window and look up. Or you can use sophisticated meteorological tools that will give a precise reading. The same is true in reading your marital climate. If you want a quick read of your climate, ask the first question under each heading in the list below, starting with "Overall." The answers to these questions will give you a quick, general read of your climate. When you have time and want a more in-depth and precise read, work through the rest of the questions.

Let's begin.

Acknowledgment
Overall, I feel that my spouse acknowledges my perspective.

    1   2   3   4   5

Consider: What topic or issue do I wish my spouse would acknowledge more?

My spouse not only acknowledges my views but welcomes them.

    1   2   3   4   5

Consider: In what topic or issue does my spouse acknowledge my view, but not necessarily welcome it?

My views are generally met with empathy rather than detached neutrality.

    1   2   3   4   5

Consider: Is there an issue where my spouse acknowledges my view but doesn't show a lot of empathy toward me?

When interacting with my spouse, I generally feel that he or she relates to me as a unique person (I-Thou) rather than merely as a spouse (I-You).

    1   2   3   4   5

Consider: Is there any aspect of the relationship where I feel taken for granted?

My spouse regularly catches me doing what's right.

    1   2   3   4   5

Consider: Do I feel that my spouse regularly notices and compliments me for what I contribute to the marriage?

Trust

Overall, I trust my spouse.

1   2   3   4   5

Consider: What does my spouse do that makes it easy for me to trust her or him?

I trust that my spouse is committed to telling me the truth.

1   2   3   4   5

Consider: Are there topics about which I suspect my spouse is being less than truthful?

I trust that the questions my spouse asks are genuine, not counterfeit questions that are designed to trap me.

1   2   3   4   5

Consider: Are there topics I have become hesitant to discuss because I am fearful of walking into a trap?

I trust that my spouse cares about and looks out for my personal welfare.

1   2   3   4   5

Consider: Are there actions or activities that my spouse does that make me feel less secure (financial risk, unhealthy friendships, broken trust)?

I trust that the values my spouse talks about in public are ones he strives to maintain in his personal life.

1   2   3   4   5

Consider: What values do I hear my spouse discuss in front of friends or family that I see her living out consistently?

Commitment

Overall, I am committed to my marriage as my highest priority (outside of fidelity to God).

1	2	3	4	5

Consider: Is there any other relationship (kids, parents, friends) or aspiration (career, material) that competes with my marriage relationship being my top priority?

When we face struggles in our marriage, I am worried that our marriage could be unstable.

1	2	3	4	5

Consider: Is there a back-door exit to the marriage if it gets too demanding?

I look back on our past and generally feel a sense of pride in how we have gone through struggles.

1	2	3	4	5

Consider: If I had a chance to go back and rewrite the history of my marriage, how much rewriting would I do?

In terms of investments—energy, thoughts, time—we generally put the same amount into the marriage.

1	2	3	4	5

Consider: Is there one aspect of my marriage that seems lopsided in terms of investments?

In terms of investments, we try to balance both of our preferences of what it means to invest in our marriage.

1	2	3	4	5

Consider: What communicates most to me that my spouse is investing in our marriage?

Expectations
Overall, my marital expectations are being met.

1   2   3   4   5

Consider: Am I comfortable with how words like *husband* or *wife* are currently being defined within my marriage?

Within reason, my spouse is meeting my relational needs.

1   2   3   4   5

Consider: How would expectations of my spouse change if we went from a community of two to belonging to a supportive larger community?

My marriage makes me feel better about myself.

1   2   3   4   5

Consider: In what two or three ways do I specifically feel better about myself because I'm married to my spouse?

I feel free to voice my expectations to my spouse.

1   2   3   4   5

Consider: What unspoken expectations do I have that are being unmet?

I generally agree with how our evolving lists of expectations (see chapter three) are being resolved.

1   2   3   4   5

Consider: What resolutions on our list (who drives carpool, who helps with homework) am I least pleased with and would I like to revisit?

COMMON QUESTIONS

When people first start to learn how to take a reading of their marital climate, several questions usually come up.

Do I add up the numbers to see if I have a positive or negative climate? No. The goal of taking a read of your marital climate isn't to find a magic number that tells you if your climate is healthy or not. Taking a reading of your climate is more art than science. There are several goals. First, in a hurrysick world, taking a reading helps us to slow down long enough to intentionally reflect on our marriage. Second, the above questions are designed to help us focus on the overall climate, not just one aspect of it. While it's important to determine if you feel valued by your spouse, it's also key to gauge if you are taking time to acknowledge him or her, investing time in the marriage daily and meeting expectations.

If the goal isn't to find a number, how will I know when we have a healthy climate? The short answer is, when you and your spouse *both* feel valued in the marriage, the climate will be considered healthy. A communication climate is the overarching sense of value and satisfaction individuals feel as they interact with each other and go about daily activities. If as you and your spouse work through these questions you both agree that you are acknowledging each other, committed to the marriage, establishing and meeting expectations and have a secure foundation of trust, you can be assured that your climate is healthy. The key to a healthy marital climate is the word *both*; for a climate to be healthy, both spouses must agree that it is mutually satisfying.

Is it possible to be doing well in only one or two areas and still have a fairly healthy climate? Yes. Remember, *acknowledgment* is perhaps the most powerful form of affirmation we can give to another person. So, if you are struggling yet you take time to acknowledge the feelings, hurt and perspective of your spouse, it will significantly improve a climate and foster a sense of value between you. This acknowledgment, in turn, allows you as a couple to address the other key elements of your marital climate.

I would also add that if *commitment* is solidified, an otherwise turbulent climate can be turned around dramatically. During the last day of marriage conferences, I ask couples to renew wedding vows to each other. I tell them that the first step in solidifying their marriage is recommitting to a future together. Taking away doubt concerning commitment provides couples with a climate that is secure and healthy enough that productive conversation addressing issues of trust, acknowledgment and expectations can occur.

Is it possible to misread my climate? Sure. After all, weather experts get forecasts wrong all the time. One of the difficulties with taking a read of your marriage is that it is based on your *perception*, and perceptions can be skewed. For example, after a passionate disagreement, you might take a reading of your climate and feel that *every* area of your climate is lacking. It's probably best to let your emotions settle a little and then take a reading. Also, it's important to take into account what else is going on in your life at the time (struggles at work, issues with the kids, financial stress) that may color your view of your relationship with your spouse.

During one month, I was experiencing daily conflict with coworkers, and I said to Noreen during dinner, "I know we've been struggling lately." Noreen responded, "We have?" I had allowed my struggles at work to influence my view of our relationship. This is why an important part of taking a reading of your marriage is checking your perceptions with your spouse. If you have different readings, it's time to listen to each other and find out where the misreading is happening and why.

How often should I take a reading of our climate? While there is no harm in regularly thinking about how you are relating to the four areas of a communication climate, be careful about how much you talk about your climate with your spouse. Again, women usually foster connection through face-to-face interaction, while men prefer closeness through activity. In other words, women generally love to talk about the relationship, while men would rather skip the talking and *do* something. For women more than men, there tends to be a temptation to take readings of the climate constantly and to want to discuss perceptions. One of the main functions of taking a reading of your climate is to determine if the climate can support having a productive conversation about a key issue in the marriage. The goal of taking a reading of the climate is *not* merely to talk about the climate.

None of us will be asked to give a forecast that could determine the outcome of an invasion and turn the tide in a world conflict, as was J. M. Stagg. Yet as couples interested in having healthy, supportive climates, we need to become just as proficient as Stagg in reading the current climate surrounding our marriage.

THINK IT OVER

1. Take a quick read of your marriage (that is, just ask the first question under each heading on pages 85-88). How do you feel about the overall climate between you and your spouse? What element of your climate do you feel most positive about? Is there an area that concerns you?

2. Set aside twenty to thirty minutes to take an in-depth reading of your marital climate by working through all the questions. How do you feel about the overall climate of your marriage? What element of your climate did you feel most positive about? Is there an area that concerns you? Did taking an in-depth reading of your climate cause you to get a different reading?

3. Is there anything going on in your life (struggles at work, stress, disagreements with coworkers) that would cause you to misread your climate with your spouse?

4. In the next day or so, consider sensitively checking your perception of the climate with your spouse.

Calling a Truce

The truce started with one unexpected act of bravery. A young German officer tired of the savagery of World War I wanted to celebrate Christmas in peace. He set down his rifle, stood up and began to walk toward the enemy on a frigid Christmas Eve night. In broken English, he shouted, "Gentlemen, my life is in your hands, for I am out of my trench and walking towards you. Will one of your officers come out and meet me half-way?"[1]

The young, cold British soldiers on the other side looked on in disbelief. Was he insane? Did he want to die? What kind of German trick was this? Finally, a British officer took his pistol out of his holster and handed it to a shocked friend, took a deep breath and stepped out of the trench. As the two soldiers walked toward each other, hundreds of rifles from both sides pointed at each other, waiting for a reason to shoot.

No provocation came. Instead, what transpired was an unlikely two-week truce that included soldiers from both sides meeting in "No Man's Land" to sing Christmas carols, share food, place haggard Christmas trees along bloody trenches, organize impromptu soccer matches and even exchange gifts. The truce did not merely create conditions in which they refrained from shooting at each other; it changed the climate so they could interact positively.

The first six chapters of *Marriage Forecasting* provided you with the tools not only to take a reading of your marital climate and but also to change your climate. What is necessary now is time to strengthen your overall climate which, in turn, will allow you to have productive conversations. A common mistake couples make is acting on impatience; they start to address the overall climate of their marriage, only to abandon that goal when a particular issue comes up that they feel must be addressed. Unfortunately, the conversation doesn't go well, and the climate suffers, making future conversations even less productive. As one scriptural proverb states, an offended person is "more unyielding than a fortified city" (18:19).

This is a vicious cycle that traps many couples. As it was for the soldier on that Christmas Eve during World War I, the first step will be the most challenging, yet can yield rewarding results.

WHAT IS A MARITAL TRUCE?

A marital truce is a conscious decision to cease hostilities with your spouse. All of us have at some point in our marriage experienced storm clouds setting in and the climate becoming difficult. Our schedules get out of control, acknowledgment of each other becomes sparse, expectations go unmet, our commitment to each other starts to be questioned, and the trust that we are a priority is slowly undermined. All of this results in a communication climate that is strained and getting worse. Daily discussions, even about small things, end in disagreements and arguments. A marital truce is *the decision to temporarily avoid controversial issues and overlook the offensive actions of each other as you seek to strengthen the overall climate of your marriage.*

One of the reasons the unlikely truce worked among the Germans and the British is that they had a common goal: celebrating Christmas. The goal of calling a truce with your spouse is to create a positive climate so that you can have productive conversations. A marital truce has two equally important parts that help establish a healthy communication climate: overlooking an offense and creating positive moments.

Overlooking an offense. The book of Proverbs has much to say about the timing of when and how we choose to address issues.

- "A fool shows his annoyance at once, but a prudent man overlooks an insult" (12:16).

- "A man finds joy in giving an apt reply—and how good is a timely word" (15:23).

- "A man's wisdom gives him patience; it is to his glory to overlook an offense" (19:11).

- "A prudent man sees danger and takes refuge, but the simple keep going" (22:3).

- "A word aptly spoken is like apples of gold in settings of silver" (25:11).

- "Do you see a man who speaks in haste? There is more hope for a fool than for him" (29:20).

Notice how much value these ancient writers place on resisting saying what you are feeling or thinking at a particular moment. It is the fool who shows his or her "annoyance at once," while the wise man "overlooks an insult" (12:16). It's not that these proverbs are asking you to repress or ignore what you are feeling. Rather, they place a strong emphasis on timing. A word spoken in the right setting is compared to a jeweler expertly placing apples of gold into settings of silver (see 25:11).

The goal of calling a truce is to create, like a wise communicator or a master artist, the right circumstances and setting to address key issues in your marriage. Even during the World War I truce, a nervous soldier occasionally took a potshot at the enemy. Wisely, the errant shot was overlooked, cooler heads prevailed, and the truce held. During your marital truce, your spouse will let loose a sarcastic comment or raise her or his voice in the heat of the moment. At that moment, you'll have to make a decision: to break the truce and respond in kind, or to overlook that offense as the proverbs suggest?

When the climate of your marriage is healthy and the time is right, you can carefully revisit issues in your marriage. The alternative is to rush in and address issues with your spouse in a communication climate that simply cannot support it. A wise person not only sees the danger ahead but alters his course accordingly (see Proverbs 22:3). To recognize that your marital climate is turbulent and still try to force a conversation is foolish. As one expert on the Proverbs notes, "Even to say the right thing at the wrong time is counterproductive."[2]

Create positive moments. Notice that after the wartime truce was called between the German and British soldiers, they did things to strengthen the truce to make sure it would hold. Each time they sang a carol, the truce grew stronger.

Just as the soldiers found ways to encourage each other, you'll have to find ways to encourage your spouse during this time of rebuilding. Marriage expert John Gottman advises couples seeking to strengthen their marriage to follow a simple mathematical formula: "You must have at least five times as many positive as negative moments together if your marriage is to be stable."[3]

The good news is that by a positive moment, Gottman means simple acts such as touching each other, smiling when your spouse comes into the room, leaving a greeting on a Post-It note, paying a compliment, saying "thank you," asking your spouse if he or she wants some ice cream when you scoop yourself some, offering to help, giving a back rub, making eye contact when your spouse is talking, calling when you're going to be late, emptying the dishwasher, saying "good morning" and "good night," sending a text asking how the day is going. You get the idea. Many of the things above—paying a compliment, sending a quick text, smiling or making eye contact, calling when you know you'll be late—take thirty seconds or less, yet they all count as positive moments! Gottman does not care what you do; he only cares that you have five positive interactions for every negative one. Most of us would think we are doing well if we do twice as many positives for every negative, and doing positively divine if we triple the positives over the negatives. Based on his years of observing thousands of couples, Gottman is unyielding in his insistence that the ratio must be 5:1. "One way to think of a stable couple is as a stereo system in which five times as much power is emitted from the positive loudspeaker as from the negative one."[4]

I must admit that the times I have tried to apply Gottman's ratio have been surprisingly convicting. To start my day with the idea that I'm going to monitor how much I'm seeking to encourage Noreen throughout the day challenges how I organize my priorities. Is the day filled with my agenda and needs, or am I making room to focus on her needs? Or, to use Gottman's language, when Noreen tunes into my stereo system, how much positive feedback is she receiving through my verbal and nonverbal communication as compared to negative static? Before I head off to work in the morning, what two or three things can I do to encourage her? Instead of just making enough coffee for me, do I make enough so she can have a cup? If the dishes in the dishwasher are clean, can I take a few extra minutes and put them away? Can I bring in the morning paper and have it sitting on the counter ready for Noreen to read? How about a quick note left by the phone: "Have a nice day!"

When I'm upset with Noreen or we've just started a truce, I seldom feel like ministering to her. So I find it necessary to say a short prayer and make an attitude adjustment. While in the midst of a truce, a 5:1 ratio of positive to negative interactions can dramatically alter our climate.

Objection to Calling a Truce

When I share this idea with couples, I often encounter a common objection: what if I want to call a truce but my spouse doesn't? After all, the German officer was met halfway by his British counterpart.

While it's best if both of you participate in the truce, the Scriptures give clear direction and hope for pursuing a truce even if your spouse doesn't. The apostle Paul writes that we should bless, rather than curse, those who act inappropriately toward us and that we should strive to live at peace with all individuals (see Romans 12:14, 18). In classical Greek, the word *bless* meant speaking well of a person. Paul goes on to say that when a person being antagonistic toward you has a need, you should respond to that need regardless of his actions. Paul states that "in doing this, you will heap burning coals on" his head (v. 20). Most Bible scholars agree that burning coals are a metaphor for the pangs of shame and remorse caused by the convicting work of the Holy Spirit initiated through the actions of the believer.

What Paul is advocating is wildly counterintuitive. When your adversary is hungry and thirsty, she or he is also vulnerable and can be exploited. Paul argues that this momentary vulnerability should be ignored and that food and drink should be offered graciously instead. Notice that Paul is not merely advocating that you refrain from doing evil; rather, you should do good by providing assistance. When you do so, God will heap burning coals on the person's head, perhaps resulting in remorse and repentance.

I know firsthand what these burning coals feel like. A few years ago, Noreen and I were in the midst of an argument that had been going on for a few days. We couldn't see eye to eye on an issue, and our climate was downright frosty. I had to leave for a local speaking engagement, and I remember saying good-night to the boys and barely mumbling a goodbye to Noreen. While I was away, Noreen decided enough was enough, called a truce in her heart and decided to pray for me.

When I returned home—fully intending to continue the silent treatment—I walked through the door to be greeted by Noreen, who hugged me and kissed me on the cheek. I strongly felt the conviction of the Spirit and knew it was time to address what was happening in our climate. What ensued was a lengthy discussion and a decision to address our hectic schedule and to apply the principles in this book.

If you decide to call a truce in your marriage, but your spouse will not, know that God will honor your decision. The easiest thing we can do in our marriage is to slip into a pattern where we treat our spouse only as he or she treats us. Yet that's not what the Scriptures call us to. The command to bless those who curse us is as shocking today as it was when Jesus first said it (see Luke 6:28). Most certainly this is also why Paul found it necessary to remind his readers not to "become weary in doing good" (Galatians 6:9).

Each time you seek to establish a truce with your spouse or to meet his or her need regardless of the response, God will honor your faithfulness, and the Spirit will use your kind actions to convict and perhaps alter your spouse's perspective. However, your actions cannot always guarantee a change on your spouse's part. What can be guaranteed is that "the eyes of the Lord are on the righteous and his ears are attentive to their prayer" (1 Peter 3:12).

PITFALLS OF A MARITAL TRUCE
Falling in love with the truce. In the blues song "Slow Dance," a husband and wife have been arguing and fussing at each other

all night. Eventually, the husband has a decision to make: does he continue to press his point of view or take a break and ask his wife to dance? He chooses to invite her to dance, and things gradually simmer down between them. This husband's instincts are good: instead of continuing to argue, let's remember why we like each other. The temptation will be for this couple to ignore the issues that lead to their arguing and just keep dancing. After experiencing conflict, tension and occasional raised voices, it's easy to become enamored with the peace and quiet produced by a truce.

However, the truce is not the goal. The goal is to create a climate where you can effectively address and resolve the issues that necessitated the truce in the first place. The temptation will be to let the truce linger week after week, thus leaving important relational issues unresolved. During a truce, it is important to regularly take a reading of your marriage to determine when the truce has done its work and the climate is strong enough to speak "the truth in love" (Ephesians 4:15). Remember, a wise person finds joy in giving a timely response (see Proverbs 15:23).

Overwhelming your spouse once the truce is over. Another pitfall of a truce is that the time can be spent creating an imposing list of grievances you want to confront your spouse with once the climate is healthy. If that happens, your spouse will view a truce as the lull before the marital storm. This is not to say that during a truce you shouldn't be prayerfully considering what issues need to be discussed once the climate is healthy and your relationship is more intimate.

Christian author and pastor Chris Brauns has two criteria concerning whether we should confront or not confront another person. First, before confronting, ask, "How important is this?" In chapter nine, we'll discuss the important skill of agenda setting, in which couples select and seek to resolve one issue at a time. Asking the question "How important is this?" helps you narrow the list of what is really important. Brauns writes, "We all know someone who thinks every offense is a big deal. We each need to evaluate ourselves and see if we are too sensitive."[5]

If during times of a marital truce everything our spouse does warrants confrontation when the truce ends, maybe we've become too sensitive and need to reevaluate what really matters to us. A helpful way of determining if something is really important is to ask, "If I could address only one or two issues with my spouse once the truce ends, what would they be?"[6] Would the issue I'm upset about right now be significant a week from now?

Second, Brauns suggests that we ask before confronting, "Does this person show a pattern of this kind of behavior?" For example, if during a truce your spouse shows up late for a family function, you may not necessarily choose to confront him or her once the truce is over if this is an isolated behavior. "If the person is perpetually late, then you may want to point out that he is cultivating a selfish habit."[7] In times of truce, it's wise to give grace to the person who acts out of character and to try to find out what factors or pressures caused your spouse to renege on a commitment or forget an important date. It's the selfish pattern that needs to be addressed once the climate is strong enough for you to speak the truth in love, not the isolated act.

Years after World War I, reporters and historians who wanted to learn more about the unlikely Christmas truce were surprised how vividly participants of the truce remembered details. British and German soldiers alike could remember the names of counterparts they had celebrated with and even the strange-sounding names of towns they had grown up in. They remembered what they ate, the songs they sang, the scores of the soccer games and the jokes they told. Many of them still had makeshift gifts exchanged on that bitterly cold Christmas. While all of them were eventually forced to go back to fighting,[8] the participants of this unlikely outbreak of peace said it forever changed how they felt toward each other. The acts of kindness and moments of peace experienced during those two weeks of truce would never be forgotten. So it will be with acts of kindness and positive moments you and your spouse will create during times of truce coupled with the work of the Spirit.

THINK IT OVER

1. The writer of Proverbs states that "a fool shows his annoyance at once, but a prudent man overlooks an insult" (12:16). Why do you think it's so hard sometimes to call a marital truce and overlook a spouse's offense?

2. John Gottman states that for a couple to strengthen their marriage they must have at least five times as many positive as negative moments together. Make a list of positive things (saying "thank you," emptying the dishwasher, holding hands) you can do for your spouse this week to strengthen your communication climate. Make a list of negative interactions that you know discourage your spouse (sarcasm, leaving dirty clothes on floor, not emptying the dishwasher), and try to avoid them in the upcoming week.

3. If you have decided to call a truce but your spouse will not, how will knowing that "the eyes of the Lord are on the righteous and his ears are attentive to their prayer" (1 Peter 3:12) help you in keeping the truce? In the days or weeks ahead, commit this verse to memory, and use it to guide you as you pray for your marriage.

Changing How We View Conflict

*W*e hadn't planned for this.

Our travel bag was packed with snacks, a map of local tourist spots, beach towels and enough sunscreen to protect a small army. But there we were, standing at our hotel room window, looking out at rain. My wife and I had this unique opportunity to go to Oahu, Hawaii, on a business trip. During the three days of meetings, we experienced glorious sunshine. When the meetings were over and it was time for us to go sightseeing, storm clouds rolled in. The locals told us that even in paradise it can get wet and chilly.

The same is true of your marital climate. No matter how diligent you and your spouse are to acknowledge each other, foster trust, create realistic expectations, commit to each other and call a truce to work on your relationship, your climate will be stormy from time to time. In other words, when two imperfect people come together, conflict will always be part of the equation.

Sometimes we think that because we profess to be followers of Christ, we should be exempt from marital conflict. We must keep in mind that even though we have embraced Christ

and have experienced his forgiveness and grace, sin is still a
lingering reality. The Scriptures are quick to remind us that
"if we claim to be without sin, we deceive ourselves and the
truth is not in us" (1 John 1:8). While all of us desire to have
a marriage that honors God, the reality of sin and the lingering effects of the fall challenge our intentions and open the
door for potential conflict.[1] "We must never be naïve enough
to think of marriage as a safe harbor from the Fall. . . . The
deepest struggles of life occur in the most primary relationship affected by the Fall: Marriage."[2]

You and your spouse can take great comfort in a conclusion
scholars draw about the inevitability of conflict: "we should
cease our efforts to find perfect people and learn how to man-
age the conflicts we are sure to have with those closest to us."[3]
Isn't that liberating? It means that if you and your spouse argue,
it's to be expected. The biggest response we get from the audience at our marriage conference is when Noreen and I have
couples turn to each other and say, "We argue too!" You should
hear the roar that goes up. Sometimes it's a challenge to get
them to quiet down. Why? Because Christian couples have an
overly spiritual idea that it's ungodly to have conflict or that
conflict is unproductive.

DEFINING CONFLICT
While there are thousands of books on conflict, few authors
take time to define what they mean by conflict. In our rush to
resolve conflict, we fail to understand what it is. The following
definition is helpful because it breaks up conflict into manage-
able sections: "Conflict is an expressed struggle between at
least two interdependent parties who perceive incompatible
goals, scarce rewards, and interference from the other party in
achieving their goals."[4] Each part of this definition warrants
our attention.

Conflict is an *expressed struggle* between at least two interdependent parties who perceive incompatible goals, scarce
rewards, and interference from the other party in achieving their goals.

Expressed struggle. From a communication standpoint, conflict exists only if it is recognized or expressed by those involved. Communicating that you are upset with someone can
be done through either verbal ("I'm angry with you," "What
you said upset me") or nonverbal (angry looks, stern tone of
voice, avoiding eye contact) ways.

One of the traps Noreen and I fall into is one of us becoming upset with the other but not expressing it to the other.
For example, one week Noreen and I had been shuttling the
boys to what seemed like a million different sporting games
and practices. While we let our boys play only one sport at a
time, it was that crazy point of the season when one sport
was ending and another was starting up, creating a tempo-
rary overlap. The color-coded pick-up/drop-off schedule on
our refrigerator looked like something designed by an air
traffic controller.

Noreen and I were exhausted, irritable and desperately waiting for Saturday morning, when nothing was scheduled and we
could finally sleep in. That was, until we realized Friday afternoon that one of us had to be at a parents' meeting early Saturday, which had been set up months before. After thinking about
it, I decided to let my wife sleep in and go. Sound good? Everything went fine until I pulled out of our driveway and my attitude started to sour. *Why did I have to go? My week was just as
long and tiring as hers, yet she's asleep. This is not fair!*

The problem was, when I got home, I spent the rest of the
day avoiding Noreen and withdrawing from her emotionally.
When she would ask what was wrong, I would reply, "Nothing."

Communication scholars call this the neglect response to conflict. This response temporarily minimizes problems, disagreements, anger or tension. People with this response prefer to keep an issue to themselves rather than start a disagreement or risk conflict. While it may be occasionally appropriate when an issue isn't important to the relationship, the problem with not expressing conflict is that the communication climate will decline when tension has not been addressed and productive conversation is avoided.[5]

> Conflict is an expressed struggle between at least two interdependent parties who *perceive incompatible goals*, scarce rewards, and interference from the other party in achieving their goals.

Perceived incompatible goals. We often view conflict through the lens of winners and losers. If you get what you want, it will come at my expense. Often in a win-lose orientation, only two positions are offered, and battle lines are quickly drawn between combatants. The forcefulness in which people will adhere to a position often takes even them by surprise.

I was once speaking to a group of engaged couples about the importance of compatibility in general, but especially compatibility in religious beliefs. After the talk, a couple came up holding hands and told me that while they enjoyed what I had to say, they disagreed about my thoughts on religious beliefs. "We come from two totally different faith traditions, and it's not been a problem at all," they said. "In the morning we go to his synagogue and at night, my church."

I told them that seemed reasonable and then asked if they wanted to have children. "Oh, yes," they said.

I asked, "In which tradition will you raise the children?"

Without missing a beat, in unison, they each said their own specific tradition. There was an awkward pause. They looked at each other and slowly stopped holding hands. She started tearing up.

While compromise is always an option for this couple (agreeing to choose one faith tradition over the other, finding a nondenominational place of worship), conflict flourishes when individuals perceive only an either-or outcome. For this couple to survive, they'd have to adopt a win-win approach in which the goal would be to find a solution that both would find satisfactory.

Conflict is an expressed struggle between at least two interdependent parties who perceive incompatible goals, *scarce rewards*, and interference from the other party in achieving their goals.

Scarce rewards. Conflict is also fostered when spouses believe there is a shortage of a particular psychological, emotional or material resource in the marriage. Relationship experts Kathryn Rettig and Margaret Bubolz identified seven resources that couples value in marriage: love, status, service, information, goods, money and shared time.[6] Dissatisfaction and conflict occur when individuals perceive a shortage in one or more areas. As you look at their list, consider: what area or resource in it is the strongest for you as a couple? Are there areas that may be lagging behind or suffering a shortage?

Noreen and I often feel that hurrysickness—living in a constant state of overdrive—continues to be a challenge for us as a couple. In the midst of my attempt to juggle work, kids, travel and church, Noreen can start to feel that the resources of *time* (he is either at work or with the boys at a game or practice) and *information* (his friends at these sporting events sometimes know more about what's going on in his life than I do) are being depleted. When our schedule is out of control, Noreen can even feel that she has to compete for the resource of *status*; she is more important than work, kids and schedules. Rettig and Bubolz's list of relational resources offers a simple and effective way for you and your spouse to determine how ripe you are for conflict.

Conflict is an expressed struggle between at least two interdependent parties who perceive incompatible goals, scarce rewards, and *interference from the other party* in achieving their goals.

Interference from the other party. "However antagonistic they might feel, the people in a conflict are dependent upon each other. The welfare and satisfaction of one depends on the actions of the others."[7] Most of us dream of having a marriage and a home that is a sanctuary from the cultural forces that press in against us. In the entrance of our home, we have a plaque that reads, "Happy is the home that shelters a friend." My goal is to have a home that serves as a shelter to me, my family and our friends. The realization of that goal is dependent on my relationship with Noreen. A scriptural proverb graphically state that "a quarrelsome wife is like a constant dripping" (19:13), and Noreen could, if she wanted, block my ability to create the type of home I envision. After all, who wants to stay in a house and be constantly dripped on?

In turn, Noreen needs me to cooperate in creating the type of family life she's always desired. Early in our marriage, we realized that every decision we made individually directly influenced each other (my going out to play basketball with the guys meant she'd stay home and watch our boys). No wonder the apostle Paul diligently reminds his readers to "look not only to your own interests, but also to the interests of others" (Philippians 2:4).

CHANGING HOW WE VIEW CONFLICT

"What's the first word you think of when I say the word *conflict*?" At marriage conferences, I have the audience shout out their answers to me. Before I tell you what my conferees most often say, in the space below, write down five words that you most readily associate with the word *conflict*:

1.

2.

3.

4.

5.

Are the words you've written negative, positive or neutral? Through the years, the most common responses from people are *war, hate, battle, lose, argument, rejection, pain, sadness, anger* and *failure*. No wonder we avoid conflict. Yet we can change how we think about conflict. First, is it possible that occasional conflict in our marriages is a good thing and can greatly strengthen our overall marital climate? Second, motivation for resolving conflict comes from understanding that disharmony in our marriage influences how the people around us view Christ. Third, one of the reasons you and your spouse experience conflict is because spiritual forces are at play, causing tension between the two of you.

THE POSITIVE EFFECTS OF CONFLICT

In perhaps one of his most provocative statements, marriage expert John Gottman says that occasional discontent and conflict are good for a marriage, *especially* in the early years of the marriage.[8] Early in our marriage, most of us view conflict as a sign that we have somehow failed as a couple. And we may still view conflict that way. Think back to the words we most readily associate with conflict: *war, hate, battle, lose, argument, rejection, pain, sadness, anger* and *failure*. What positives could come from relational conflict?

One of the things conflict can force us to do is work on our metacommunication. The word *metacommunication* includes the prefix *meta*, meaning "about," and *communication*. So, metacommunication is simply communicating about our communication. I was once watching a sitcom with my wife in which a couple was having an argument. At one point, the boyfriend said in a flabbergasted voice, "This is the stupidest argument we've ever had! We're arguing about how we argue!" Noreen and I looked at each other and smiled because we knew better: having a passionate conversation about how you communicate is one of the most important things a couple can do—and conflict often forces you to do it.

Early in our marriage, Noreen and I didn't do well with conflict. When tension or disagreements hit our marital climate, I would evoke what is typically called the exit response. This response entails physically walking away from a person during a conflict or withdrawing from him or her psychologically or emotionally. Because I was ill-equipped to handle conflict early in our marriage, when a disagreement came up between us, I often would listen to Noreen, mumble a few words and leave the room. I would wait what I thought was an appropriate amount of time and then simply pretend nothing had happened. Needless to say, this was frustrating to Noreen and ineffective in resolving our differences.

I remember clearly the night Noreen turned off the TV, sat down next to me and said, "We need to talk about how we don't talk." Fortunately for us, our climate was at a place where I could receive what she had to say, and we began a long conversation about how to have productive conversations. The power of occasional conflict, according to Gottman, is that it brings us to the point where we *feel* the need to improve our communication. The book of Proverbs compares a heated quarrel to a dam that has been breached (see 17:14). It only takes one or two dam-bursting arguments for an emotionally drenched couple to be motivated to reevaluate their communication style, climate and conflict style.

MOTIVATION TO RESOLVE CONFLICT

In the last few hours of his life, Christ experienced personal betrayal, two hastily convened trials, scourging, public humiliation and crucifixion. To prepare, he gathered his disciples together for one last meal. This time together, commonly called the "Upper Room Discourse," contains Jesus' final instructions to them. A pivotal moment came when Jesus told his disciples, "By this all men will know that you are my disciples, if you love one another" (John 13:35). The love each of these men had experienced while following Christ would serve as a standard of Christian love. Jesus told them that the authenticity of their love for him would be judged by their mutual love for each other. "As I have loved you, so you must love one another" (v. 34). What Jesus was saying is remarkable and has implications for all of us who claim to be his followers: if you want to judge the authenticity of Christianity, look at the love and unity between Christians.

One place that this love and unity ought to be evident is in Christian marriages. In his book *Sacred Marriage*, Gary Thomas argues that one key purpose of Christian marriage is to put flesh on God's message of reconciliation, which he defines as "to end a relation of enmity, and to substitute for it one of peace and goodwill."[9] He then makes this point why resolving conflict in our marriage is so crucial: "We cannot discuss with any integrity the ending of 'a relation of enmity' and the dawning of 'peace and goodwill' if our marriages are marked by divorce, fighting, and animosity."[10]

God's great desire is to reconcile our unbelieving family members, neighbors and friends back to him, and he is going to do that, in part, through our marriages. I once heard a speaker say that the most effective evangelistic tool today is a healthy marriage, because it's a modern miracle. In a culture of divorce and starter marriages, the sight of Christian couples staying committed and working through conflict is evidence of God's power and grace. It greatly motivates Noreen and me to settle our disagreements, knowing that it's not just about us; people are watching and will judge the authenticity of Christ's love based on our marital harmony. In commenting on former vice president Al Gore's unexpected split from Tipper, his wife of forty years, *Time* magazine writer Belinda Luscombe suggests that perhaps they no longer had any big projects on their plate, obstacles to overcome or common enemies to challenge them. In short, they grew bored of each other. For Christians, our continual project is to attempt to cultivate marriages that reflect God's love, and our common enemy is a spiritual adversary vividly described in the Scriptures.[11]

SPIRITUAL FORCES

C. S. Lewis stated that two mistakes we make concerning Satan are to attribute nothing to him as if he didn't exist and to attribute everything to him. Lewis concludes that Satan is equally pleased with either error.[12] I tend to be prone not to take Satan seriously enough. In the writings of Paul, we see him acknowledging human evil but never losing sight of a higher spiritual reality at play. While he notes that there are "many who oppose me" (1 Corinthians 16:9), and he even singles out individuals such as Alexander the metalworker (see 2 Timothy 4:14), he never loses sight of the real war, which is against the "god of this age" (2 Corinthians 4:4). Paul informs his readers that "our struggle is not against flesh and blood, but against the . . . powers of this dark world" and the "spiritual forces of evil" (Ephesians 6:12).

When addressing conflict in our marriages, we would do well to maintain the balance struck by Lewis and the apostle Paul. Certainly we struggle in our marriages because we give in to anger or have had poor marital role models or lack communication skills. However, as Christian couples seeking to love each other as Christ loves us and to model to others God's message of reconciliation, we'd be naive (and unbiblical) to think that Satan does not play a role in our marital struggles.

But, you might say, we've never experienced in our marriage any dramatic attacks or anything even remotely resembling a scene out of *Paranormal Activity* or *The Exorcist*. While I'm not dismissing dramatic accounts of the supernatural (I've heard plenty of stories from credible sources), let me explain why dramatic attacks may not be Satan's favorite method of disrupting your marriage. In the Genesis account of the tempting of Adam and Eve, Satan is portrayed as a serpent and described as being "crafty," which from the Hebrew can be translated "subtle" (3:1).

As you read the Genesis narrative, you'll notice that Satan never comes out and says, "Rebel against God!" Rather, he tries to slowly undermine Eve's trust in God's words, promises and character. "Did God really say, 'You must not eat from any tree in the garden?'" the serpent says to Eve, distorting God's words (3:1). In other words, Satan tries to win small victories leading to a big fall.

Whenever I think of Satan's subtle strategies with Eve, I think back to a pivotal moment in my karate training as a teen. When you earn a third-degree green belt in Korean karate, you earn the right to spar with black belts. I'll never forget lining up across from my partner, a third-degree black belt, bowing and waiting for the signal to begin. When we got the signal, he just stood there while I bounced around. As I threw punches, which he easily blocked, he occasionally and harmlessly kicked me in the lower leg. It didn't hurt at all. As I grew more confident in my attack, he simply kicked me again in the same leg. This time it stung a little, but was only a slight nuisance. My confidence skyrocketed as I threw a combination of kicks and punches, causing him to back up slightly.

Then he did something I'll never forget. He faked a kick, causing me look down. I never saw the left hook that sent me to the mat. See what he did? He set me up. He won minor victories (harmless kicks), setting me up for the big victory (left hook). I wonder if Satan doesn't do the same with us and our marriages. He gets us so busy (hurrysickness) that we have no time to acknowledge each other. We spend so much time pursuing things (affluenza) that we start to question our commitment to each other.

How is Satan trying to set up you and your spouse? One of Satan's favorite strategies seems to come in the form of tension between spouses; unresolved conflict leads to emotional distance, which leads to resentment, which leads to bitterness, which leads to a communication climate that is cold, unloving and despairing. It would be wise to take time as a couple in the next few days to reflect on how you would answer that question. "Be alert," Peter wisely warns all of us when addressing the issue of spiritual attack (see 1 Peter 5:8).

THINK IT OVER

1. Why does it comfort us to know that marital conflict is inevitable and that other Christian couples also occasionally argue? Where did we get the idea that Christian couples shouldn't argue or experience conflict?

2. Earlier in the chapter, I asked you to write the first five words that you most readily associated with the word *conflict*. Were your words mostly negative, neutral or positive? Where did these associations come from?

3. In *Sacred Marriage*, Gary Thomas argues that one of the purposes of marriage is to spread God's love and message of reconciliation. How does knowing that God is using your marriage to influence unbelieving family members, neigh-

bors and friends change how you approach conflict between you and your spouse?

4. One of Satan's subtle tactics is to set a Christian couple up by winning small victories in preparation for the big fall. How do you think Satan is currently—and most likely subtly—setting you up for his main attack?

Seven Principles for Making Disagreements Productive

*I*t finally came to a head one evening when I was making dinner. Noreen was going out with some friends, and I was cooking the one thing I know how to make: over-easy eggs. With one egg on my spatula, I turned toward the table, and Michael held up his plate and said, "Throw it, Dad!" I thought to myself, *I can do this.* In one motion I tossed the egg. Noreen turned the corner just in time to see the egg miss the plate and hit our hardwood cabinet, splattering egg yolk everywhere. The kids gasped, and Noreen's eyes met mine with a look of *Oh no you didn't.* Without thinking, I said, "Michael told me to do it."

When it comes to dinnertime etiquette, what's permissible and what's not? This is a running disagreement Noreen and I have had since we started having kids. I like to have fun at dinner—laughing until milk rushes out of my nose fun. Noreen isn't opposed to having fun, but she wants to raise gentlemen. She's terrified at the thought of our boys eating in public or at other people's homes. This one issue—what's appropriate behavior at the dinner table—has caused more turbulence in our climate than any other issue. Really, consider how often you eat dinner.

Relational experts break marital conflict into two broad categories: conflicts that can be resolved and conflicts that can't and are perpetual. One scholar estimates that the majority of marital conflicts, approximately 69 percent, are irresolvable and will be with a couple in one form or another for the life of the marriage.[1] What are the types of issues or conflicts that fall in the irresolvable, perpetual category? You are a spender; your spouse is a saver. You like to have a nice clean house; your spouse has a greater tolerance for clutter. You like to plan your vacation to the last detail; your spouse likes to be spontaneous. You are more interested in sex than your spouse is. Your spouse wants your daughter to play on a travel sports team, while you want her to focus more on school. What makes these issues irresolvable is that no one is clearly wrong or right. Psychologist Dan Wile summarizes the perpetual nature of conflict: "When choosing a long-term partner . . . you will inevitably be choosing a particular set of unsolvable problems that you'll be grappling with for the next ten, twenty, or fifty years."[2]

What makes grappling with these reoccurring problems so difficult is the tendency to push back against our spouse's attempt to resolve the issue in her or his favor. For instance, the more Noreen tries to establish manners at the dinner table, the more I push back and become more carefree. The more she sees me goofing off, the firmer she is with etiquette. Meanwhile, the communication climate diminishes, making it harder to talk effectively about our differences.

In this chapter I'll use our reoccurring struggle with dinnertime behavior as a test case to work through seven principles that can help you address the issues that keep popping up to disrupt your marital climate.

PRINCIPLE 1: DO A CONFLICT ASSESSMENT

The actions we take after a disagreement and before we try to resolve the issue will largely determine the outcome. Key to our preparation is what experts who study conflict call conflict assessment. This assessment is simply a set of prompts that help you slow the rush to confrontation and think about the event from many different angles, including that of your spouse. For example:

- What set the off the conflict?
- Explain the conflict from your perspective.
- Explain the conflict from the other person's perspective.
- What kinds of emotions does the conflict arouse in you?
- Why do you think you feel the way you do about the conflict?

While each of these questions is important, these two are particularly helpful: *Why do you think you feel the way you do about the conflict? Explain the conflict from the other person's perspective.*

Consider the answer to the question "Why do you think you feel the way you do about the conflict?" In my case, why is having fun at the table so important to me?

While I was growing up in East Detroit, my father often worked double shifts at General Motors just to make ends meet, leaving my mother alone with three rambunctious boys. She was outnumbered and often overwhelmed. Her one way to reel us in was to utter prophetic words of judgment: "Wait till your father comes home!" When we saw Dad's car come down the street, we'd run in the other direction and lay low. Until dinner, that is. When dinner came, there was no hiding. My brothers and I ate with the knowledge that at any moment Mom could clear her throat and say, "John, we need to have a talk about your boys." *Your boys*—never a good sign. We sat in silence as a list of grievances was offered in precise detail and duly noted by my father. When dinner was over, the sentencing phase would begin.

Now that I have three boys of my own, I can imagine the frustration we caused my mother (she started a family at twenty) and completely understand the tactics she adopted. However, when I started a family, I had a different vision for the dinner hour. I didn't want the dinner table to be primarily associated with discipline or correction. So, when Noreen starts to correct the kids concerning manners, I interpret it as her valuing discipline over camaraderie.

Why are manners so important to Noreen? To be honest, at first I didn't have a clue. I was so caught up in my own agenda that I never took time to ask. There's a proverb that says, "There is a way that seems right to a man" (Proverbs 16:25). One night, after we'd had another disagreement, I asked why it was so important for the boys to act properly at dinner. She told me exactly why.

Noreen's maiden name is Lenehan; she comes from a proud Irish family. She is one of six siblings who dearly love each other (I fondly call them the Irish Waltons). She has a vivid childhood memory of her family eating at a restaurant. As they were finishing, an elderly couple walked up and told Mr. and Mrs. Lenehan they'd been watching them the entire time. "You have such a well-mannered family. You must be so proud!"

Noreen told me, "I'll never forget the look on my parents' faces." It was at that moment that she developed a dream for her future family—a family that can enjoy each other while being well-mannered.

The value of hearing stories like this is that it can, if we allow it, produce the quality of communication Jack Gibb talks about: empathy (see chapter five). Sally Planalp, a communication scholar who explores the vital link between emotions and how we express ourselves, argues that emotions are a powerful indi-

cator of how we view the world.[3] The more powerful the emotion, the more strongly we feel that something isn't right or that
an injustice has been committed. If our emotions or perspective
is ignored, conflict resolution will become increasingly unlikely. In light of this, scholars regard empathy as the "pinnacle
of listening" and argue that empathy can facilitate successful
conflict resolution.[4]

Imagine Noreen growing up with a vivid image of what her
future family will be one day: a family that enjoys each other yet
is so well-mannered that strangers will come up to her in public
and compliment her and her husband for the parenting job they
have done. Now imagine that dream being threatened by an egg-
tossing husband who seemingly doesn't value manners. In the
previous chapter, I said that an integral part of the definition of
conflict is when spouses see each other as interfering with personal goals. What powerful emotions it must surface in Noreen
to see me as interfering with her dreams for our family!

Empathy powerfully communicates to the person with whom
you are having conflict that you care about him and the emotions the conflict is surfacing for him. Remember that defensive
climates take shape when our perspectives are met with detached
neutrality that fails to acknowledge our emotions or passions.

A significant benefit of taking time to assess conflict before
bringing it up with your spouse is that it not only allows your powerful emotions to settle but also provides you with valuable insight
and perspective about yourself and your spouse. As a proverb af-
firms, "The discerning heart seeks knowledge" (15:14).

PRINCIPLE 2: CHECK THE CLIMATE
The premise of *Marriage Forecasting* is that more communication is not always the solution to our marital problems. Before
a couple dives into delicate relational issues, they ought to place
a "Weather Permitting" sign above their heads. If the overall

communication climate of the marriage is not healthy, the chance of their conversation being productive is greatly diminished. As communication scholars McCroskey and Wheeles note, "More and more negative communication merely leads to more and more negative results."[5] After taking an assessment of the conflict, the next step is to take a reading of the climate of your marriage (see chapter six) and determine if the climate can support the type of conversation you want to have. If it can't, you need to carefully set out to improve key aspects of your climate.

PRINCIPLE 3: MAKE A DATE TO TALK

Attempts to resolve conflict often fail because one spouse confronts another who isn't ready to discuss the issue. In a hurrysick world, there are times when a spouse is too tired or distracted to effectively resolve significant differences. Setting up a time to talk has several advantages.

First, and most importantly, it allows you time to pray for the conversation. The apostle Paul states that we should, in everything, pray (see Philippians 4:6). Here's a brief list of things to pray for:

- *Insight into my contribution to the conflict.* "Search me, O God, and know my heart," prayed King David. "See if there is any offensive way in me" (Psalm 139:23-24). I honestly cannot think of one conflict between Noreen and me when I was absolved from any blame. When heading into a discussion of differences, it is wise to ask the Lord to reveal to you areas where you have contributed to the problem.

- *Protection against spiritual attack.* "Put on the full armor of God so that you can take your stand against the devil's schemes" (Ephesians 6:11). The Greek word translated as *stand* in this verse is a military term for holding a position against hostile attack. As discussed in the previous chapter, if the purpose of your marriage is to model to others Christ's love through the unity in your marriage, you can be sure you're a target for spiritual attack. That being the case, it would be wise to pray in advance for predetermined times when the goal is for you as a couple to restore unity.

• *Humility.* "When pride comes, then comes disgrace, but with humility comes wisdom" (Proverbs 11:2). Simply put, pray for humility. It is pure hubris to think that I, like Dr. Gregory House, am always right on every issue.

• *Self-control.* "A fool gives full vent to his anger, but a wise man keeps himself under control" (Proverbs 29:11). Powerful emotions are part of conflict. If we didn't feel strongly about this issue, we wouldn't be having the disagreement in the first place. However, we need to pray for wisdom regarding when to back off during the discussion or perhaps even to take a break to gain control if we feel that things are spiraling out of control emotionally or physically.

• *My spouse.* "No one ever hated his own body, but he feeds and cares for it" (Ephesians 5:29). I'll know I'm ready for our date to discuss our differences if I can pray for the well-being of the person who, according to Genesis, is one flesh with me. If I can't pray for Noreen's well-being heading into this time, I know I'm not ready—spiritually—to talk.

Second, setting up a date allows men time to gear up for something most of us would rather avoid. It's not that men are bad at conflict or that we won't take the lead and set up a date to talk about it. It's just that working out disagreements with our wives takes a physical and emotional toll on us. Studies in the field of gender have shown that one of the reasons men avoid conflict is that, during an argument, men experience intense physical and emotional reactions, such as a quickly elevated heart rate and rapid breathing that stays elevated even after the conflict ends.

In other words, the physical reactions I had as a green belt in karate waiting to fight a black belt for the first time or when preparing to engage in intense business negotiations are the same physical and emotional feelings many men experience when they have conflict with their wives. Except in karate I can physically assert myself or in negotiations I can raise my voice or aggressively assert myself, things I know I shouldn't do with my wife. Due to the physical and emotional toll conflict takes on us, men will often deny, minimize or avoid entirely any issue that could spark conflict with their wife. Setting a date to discuss a disagreement allows a man time to prepare for an event and to pray for self-control (see Proverbs 29:11).

Third, setting a date to talk allows you to set a specific agenda for that time. One of the common mistakes couples make is to start talking about one issue (the budget), only to have it bring up several semi-related issues ("I know you want to get DirectTV, but we already watch too much TV as a family!" "Whatever happened to the idea of us having family devotions?"). *Kitchen-sinking* is when spouses start to throw into the original conversation every topic they think of (everything but the kitchen sink). While this is an amusing term, it can have serious implications for men. The same gender studies that discovered men's physical reactions to conflict noted that flooding men with topics or complaints caused them to retreat or withdraw emotionally, psychologically or physically from the discussion.[6] The goal is to keep your time focused on the specific issue that is causing the conflict (the budget, not your television-watching habits).

When important side issues do come up, you can incorporate a useful technique called *bracketing*. Bracketing is purposefully acknowledging an important issue arising in a conversation and deciding to discuss it later. For example, when discussing our disagreement over dinnertime behavior, I mentioned to Noreen that I enjoyed the carefree way we interacted as a family when we ate out at fast-food establishments and wished we could incorporate that at home. Part of Noreen's response entailed a concern that eating out was putting a strain on our budget (three boys can eat *a lot*). Utilizing the concept of bracketing, I replied, "That's a fair point, and we need to discuss it. Could we agree to come back to it later?"

PRINCIPLE 4: AFFIRM THE RELATIONAL LEVEL OF COMMUNICATION
When immersed in conflict with our spouse, we tend to get hung up on the content level (who, what, when, where) and speaking truth, and we forget to stress the relational level (*I like you and am committed to you*). That's why Paul is so wise to remind us to speak the truth *in* love (Ephesians 4:15). On many occasions, when Noreen and I have set a date to work through an issue, we've headed into that time upset and convinced that the other person was wrong or not seeing the issue clearly. When we start that time by reaffirming our commitment to each other, our discussion goes smoother. By speaking "love" first, the "truth" is easier to receive.

Don't think for a moment that we start by holding hands and lovingly staring into each other's eyes. Hardly. Rather, it's a *decision* to articulate what we know to be true (we love and are committed to each other), even if we are not particularly feeling it at that moment. When we've skipped the reaffirming of our commitment and jumped into the content (speaking truth without love), the climate between us has seemed more defensive and the resolution has been slower and harder to achieve.

PRINCIPLE 5: BEGIN WITH THE THIRD STORY
Professional mediators Douglas Stone, Bruce Patton and Sheila Heen suggest that most of us make a mistake in at-

tempting to resolve conflict with another person by how we *start* a conversation:

> Often, we start from inside our own story. We describe the problem from our own perspective and, in doing so, trigger just the reactions we hope to avoid. We begin from precisely the place the other person thinks is causing the problem. If they agreed with our story, we probably wouldn't be having this conversation in the first place.[7]

These experts observe that when two people disagree, there are three stories, not two. Every conflict includes each participant's story and an invisible third story. The third story is "one a keen observer would tell, someone with no stake in your particular problem."[8] The key to starting a difficult conversation is to begin with your version of the third story. This means describing the problem between you and your spouse in a way that that rings true for *both* of you.

Telling the third story from your perspective entails risk. The third story will be effective only if you describe the problem in such a way that acknowledges the complexity and validity of your spouse's intentions, desires and goals. If the third story comes across as favoring your position, it could turn a turbulent communication climate even more negative. For example, consider the disagreement Noreen and I have over dinnertime behavior. A third story would perhaps sound like this:

> Both of us have dreams for our family that include valuing manners and fun. Each of us wants to raise boys who have discernment and understand what is and is not acceptable behavior at the dinner table. We both see dinner as a time of education and family fun. Neither of us is comfortable with how that balance is currently being played out.

If the third story is told in a manner that acknowledges the validity of both perspectives, it can be powerfully affirming to both of you and help establish a confirming communication climate. Hopefully from my third story you picked up that both Noreen and I have equally legitimate dreams; both value manners and fun, and each of us wants to raise boys who have discernment. The issue isn't that fun is more important than manners, but one of balance.

Who should tell the third story? I suggest that either you take turns (alternate each time you have a conflict) or let the spouse who has a knack for telling the fairest third story lead off with it. The third story isn't a competition; it's a way to get the conversation started in a productive manner. Research shows that you'll typically end a conversation with the same tone (harsh, affirming, sarcastic, yelling, conciliatory) as you start. The third story helps you begin the conversation with a strong note of acknowledgment, which is central to a positive communication climate. (In the "Think It Over" section, you'll get a chance to practice writing your own version of a third story.)

PRINCIPLE 6: SPEAK SUPPORTIVELY

One of the most important skills you can cultivate is monitoring your communication as you discuss issues with your spouse. Whenever I do public-speaking training with clients, the first thing I seek to accomplish is to make them aware of what they are saying and doing in front of an audience. One client would look at his wristwatch at the most inopportune times. While passionately talking about the millions of people in the world who have never heard of Christ, he'd look at his watch and then continue speaking. "John," I would say from the back row, "do you have a plane to catch?" He was never aware he did it.

If we are serious about maintaining a healthy communication climate with our spouse, we must carefully monitor our communication to see if we are slipping into negative habits. Defensive and stormy marital climates are created by evaluation, certainty, strategy, control orientation, neutrality and superiority (see chapter five). As you interact with your spouse, diligently monitor communication for signs of these unproductive habits, and be open to your spouse pointing out these traits in you. Remember, "wounds from a friend can be trusted" (Proverbs 27:6).

PRINCIPLE 7: SEEK A WIN-WIN ORIENTATION

A win-win approach assumes that if you and your spouse are willing, there is a solution to your problem that will be mutually satisfactory. At the heart of this approach is *compromise*. The term *compromise* itself originates from the Latin for "middle way." That's what a compromise is, isn't it? A middle way between the two positions currently held by you and your spouse. A middle way is what Noreen and I needed to forge in our disagreement over dinnertime behavior. A compromise meant that neither of us was going to get exactly what we wanted, and we needed to find a middle way.

After much discussion about table manners, we settled on the following win-win agreement. Whenever Noreen makes a formal dinner and we sit down as a family to eat in the dining room, the Muehlhoff men are to act appropriately. That's not to say we can't have fun, but it's a value to us as parents to raise boys who know what proper dinner decorum is. I needed to realize that adding a little correction to dinner didn't have to inhibit our fun.

It's extremely important for Noreen to know that I've bought into this decision to help the boys learn what acceptable behavior is and that I'm not just sitting by as she does her thing. Conversely, when life is too busy to have a formal dinner and we eat at the kitchen counter or eat while watching ESPN, the atmosphere can get a little crazy and a French fry or two has been known to be launched (eggs are off-limits).

To continue to maintain healthy climates by effectively addressing conflict requires that we learn to embrace God's forgiveness and pass it on to others. Each of us, sooner or later, will be in the position where we'll wrestle with the need to forgive those closest to us. As we shall see in the next chapter, granting forgiveness is often a challenge. "Everyone says forgiveness is a lovely idea," noted C. S. Lewis, "until they have something to forgive."[9]

THINK IT OVER

1. The apostle Paul states that we should, in everything, pray (see Philippians 4:6). How would diligently praying for an upcoming conversation with your spouse affect your attitude heading into the conversation? What are some of the reasons prayer is often neglected in preparing to resolve marital conflict?

2. Why is it often difficult to speak "the truth in love" when in the midst of a conflict with your spouse? How does hearing the love part first make hearing hard truths easier?

3. The key to starting a difficult conversation is to begin with your version of the third story. This means describing the problem between you and your spouse in a way that rings true for *both* of you. Think back to a recent (or current) conflict between you and your spouse, and try writing a third story that fairly represents both perspectives. When finished, give it to your spouse, and ask him or her how you did.

4. Think back to a time when you and your spouse reached a compromise that you both felt good about. If you were coaching a couple at an impasse on how to reach a compromise, what advice would you give them? In other words, what are the three or four necessary ingredients for a successful compromise?

The Necessity of Forgiveness

*A*fter writing more than forty-five complex books focusing on God, philosophy and logic, Christian philosopher Peter Kreeft wanted to write something for his kids and grandkids before his career came to an end. So, between writing academic books, he found time to scribble on pieces of paper thoughts about love, God, friendship, work and laughter. These notes resulted in the book *Before I Go: Letters to Our Children About What Really Matters*. His note on marriage is short and thought provoking: "There is never any problem, misery, or evil in any human relationship that cannot be changed or healed if only two things are present: forgiveness and determination. All the rest is nuts and bolts."[1]

There will come a time when all of us will be faced with the decision whether or not to forgive our spouse for a transgression. If you decide to forgive, you will need not only determination but also an understanding of what constitutes forgiveness, the biblical motivation to pursue it, and clear steps to ensure that forgiveness strengthens the climate between you and your spouse. Before defining forgiveness, let's consider the consequences of choosing both to forgive and not to forgive others.

THE BENEFITS OF FORGIVENESS AND THE DANGERS OF NOT FORGIVING

In his landmark study of forgiveness, Douglas Kelley noted that the nature or the severity of the offense did not determine if a particular relationship survived. After the offense, respondents in Kelley's study recorded an immediate drop in intimacy, satisfaction, relationship stability and relationship quality. However, he also found that if the forgiveness process was handled appropriately by each person in the relationship (explicit apology offered, direct expression of forgiveness granted), respondents recorded that the levels of relational satisfaction, intimacy, stability and quality not only rose to original levels, but in some cases *surpassed* old levels.[2] Why? In some cases the offense served as a wakeup call causing the spouses to focus on deficiencies in the overall marital climate. Not only was the offense (such as lying about credit card use) addressed and forgiven, but the couple also began to address other important issues (such as the need to start a budget and communicate more openly about finances). While none of us wants to be in a position of having to forgive our spouse, the act of forgiveness can strengthen a communication climate.

However, research also shows that choosing to hold on to our grudges and not forgive can threaten our personal well-being. Everett Worthington, director of the Campaign for Forgiveness Research, argues that negative emotions associated with unresolved conflict and an unforgiving attitude compromise our immune system. Worthington and his research team have sought to help, among others; mothers in Northern Ireland who have lost children to religious violence. His studies show that women who forgive these perpetrators of injustice report a reduction in symptoms of stress, including severe headaches and backaches, and the release of negative emotions.

Our refusal to forgive our spouse comes at great mental, physical and spiritual cost. Could it be that the physical aches and pains we experience regularly are residue of our refusal to forgive those closest to us?

DEFINING FORGIVENESS

While there are many detailed definitions of forgiveness, I'll offer a thin slice from the field of communication of what it means to forgive: *we forgive another when we let go of the anger, resentment, blame and other toxic feelings we have toward the offender.* Of course, forgiveness should entail both parties coming together to clear the air, talk about grievances and reach a mutual understanding of what needs to be forgiven and what constitutes forgiveness. However, a key part of forgiveness is what happens in the spirit of the offended spouse after the transgression happens.

In his book *The Art of Forgiving*, Lewis Smedes states that all individuals intent on forgiving must move through three internal stages. First, to forgive you must rediscover the humanity of the person who hurt you. Smedes suggests that the person who hurt us must move from being a monster to being a "person who shares our faulty humanity, bruised like us, faulty like us, still thoroughly blamable for what he did to us. Yet, human like us."[3] Second, you must surrender your right to get even. Smedes vividly compares the fantasy of getting even with the person who wronged you to an intravenous drip stuck into your veins, pushing spiritual poison into your system. Third, you revise your feelings toward the person who hurt you. The surest way to know that you have forgiven a person is to pray for God's blessing on her.

In the study previously mentioned, 45 percent of the participants said they had forgiven family members or spouses but still held onto grudges or negative feelings. After years of research, Kelley concluded that an understanding of forgiveness was useless unless individuals were motivated to forgive. He listed the most common reasons to forgive: a commitment to the relationship, love and fear of losing one's partner. While these are also motivations for Christian couples interested in establishing healthy marital climates, followers of Christ have another motivation to pursue forgiveness: the sacrificial life of Jesus and his command to forgive.

THE COMMAND TO FORGIVE

In his letter to the church at Ephesus, Paul gives us one of the most important commands concerning forgiveness, which has crucial implications for our marital climates. In stark terms, he tells us that we should forgive "each other, just as in Christ God forgave you" (Ephesians 4:32). Did you catch that? The central motivation for forgiving our spouse is that God forgave us. However, it is imperative that we not miss the most important part of what Paul wrote: "*in Christ* God forgave you." Our motivation to forgive our spouse will grow proportional to our understanding of what it cost Christ—emotionally, psychologically and physically—to save us. In the second chapter of Philippians, Paul gives a gripping description of what Christ went through to secure your and my salvation. The more we grasp what Paul says, the more our motivation to forgive will expand.

THE HUMILITY OF CHRIST (PHILIPPIANS 2:5-11)

As we consider Philippians 2:5-11, notice how the level of humility and shame Christ experienced deepens, and ask yourself, *Why is he allowing himself to be treated like this?*

Humbled as a man. Paul starts by saying that although Jesus was "in very nature God" (v. 6) he didn't hang on to all the rights and privileges of being God when he came to our planet.

Think about it. If he came to earth as the God described in Isaiah 6 (constantly surrounded by angels proclaiming, "Holy, holy, holy") or Revelation 1 (eyes blazing like fire and a voice booming like raging waters), how could we interact with him? Rather, he "made himself nothing" (v. 7) and humbled himself with a human body. Imagine that. God with human limitations. The God who created the universe now has to travel by foot, eat, sleep on the floor, be bathed as an infant, be protected as a child from humans he created and so on.

Humbled as a servant. It would be understandable if God came to this planet as a king with full royal privileges. Yet Paul says that Jesus took the form of a "servant" (v. 7). Jesus didn't come to grab headlines or to mix with politicians or the power elite. When he came across the hungry, he fed them; when the sick were brought to him, he healed them. His followers didn't wash his feet, he washed theirs. We are encouraged when our leaders roll up their sleeves and humbly serve their constituents; we are awed when God comes among us and serves.

Humbled by death. This is where Christianity gets a little crazy for some. We believe not only that God visited our planet two thousand years ago but also that, motivated by love, he willingly died for us. "And being found in appearance as a man, he humbled himself and became obedient to death" (v. 8).

Humbled by death on a cross. "Obedient to death—even death on a cross" (v. 8). The fact that Jesus died on a cross is why some of Paul's listeners considered the gospel to be foolishness (see 1 Corinthians 1:18, 23). For many in Paul's day, it made no sense to worship a crucified criminal. How could individuals revere as a god a man who had been judged a criminal and been subjected to a humiliating and barbaric form of execution?

When the Romans began using crucifixion as a form of execution, it had clear limits: the individual being crucified must
be a foreigner or slave convicted of murder, rebellion or armed
robbery. The idea of a Roman being crucified was unthinkable.
The Roman statesman Cicero described crucifixion as "a most
cruel and disgusting punishment."[4] He continued, "To bind a
Roman citizen is a crime, to flog him is an abomination, to kill
him is almost an act of murder: to crucify him is—what? There
is no fitting word that can possibly describe such a horrible
deed."[5] Yet the reason Christ subjected himself to a death so
beneath a Roman citizen was to secure our salvation, a salvation in which our sins (past, present and future) have been
dealt with by God the Father in Christ.

What should be our response to such divine humility? For
Chuck and Melissa, the answer to that question saved their
marriage.

Though he was off duty when a bomb ripped apart the Alfred P.
Murrah Federal Building in downtown Oklahoma City, Chuck
was one of the first officers to arrive on the scene on April 19,
1995. He walked into what had been the daycare facility and
remembers finger paint sticking to his boots. The nightmare
images of that scene worsened his drinking and bouts of anger,
and sent an already unstable marriage into crisis. Separated
from his wife, depressed and seeking to reconnect with God
and his family, Chuck begged Melissa to attend a FamilyLife
marriage conference. She finally agreed, only because she
thought that the communication skills she'd learn would help
her in her *next* marriage.

Noreen and I happened to be speaking at the conference
Chuck and Melissa attended, and we met up with them after a
session in which the gospel had been presented. It was obvious
God had been working in both of them, and during that conversation Melissa embraced Christ as her Savior. While both of

them were excited about what God was doing, little did they know that once the conference was over, their slowly warming marital climate would be severely tested.

After the conference was over, Chuck drove Melissa to her mother's house, where he sat her down on the couch. "If this marriage is going to work," he began, "I need to come clean." He proceeded to tell Melissa of multiple acts of unfaithfulness. When she couldn't hear any more, she ran to the bathroom and closed the door. Sick to her stomach, she prayed, "God, I've been a Christian for seventy-two hours. I can't do this!" All she could do was sit on the floor and wait for a response. She later recounted,

> The only way I can explain what happened next is to say that I was flooded with an understanding of how much God had forgiven me. *Everything, forgiven.* Now, in this moment, the Lord was asking me to take a piece of that forgiveness and give it to my husband. As I walked back from the bathroom to the living room, I made the decision to pass on God's forgiveness.

Though Melissa didn't know the verse at the time, she was living out Paul's admonition "[Forgive] each other, just as in Christ God forgave you" (Ephesians 4:32).

Though Melissa made the decision to forgive Chuck that evening, letting go of pain and anger and rebuilding trust would take time. On some days she was overcome with insecurity or pain and had to call Chuck to talk it out. On some occasions she had the strong impression that her anger was being stirred up by spiritual forces intent on attacking her commitment to her marriage. While few of us will experience such a drastic challenge to our marital climate, all of us need to be aware of the steps of forgiveness Melissa had to walk through to finally let go of her anger and forgive.

STEPS TOWARD FORGIVENESS

First step: Commit to a way of life that makes forgiveness possible. Melissa's ability to forgive a husband who had been unfaithful was dependent on adopting a new way of life rooted in God's power and grace. While the decision to forgive was made on her knees in her mother's bathroom, the ability to follow through was dependent on daily prayer, reading and meditating on the Scriptures, and on being immersed in a community of believers. Christian author Dallas Willard makes this convincing argument:

> My central claim is that we *can* become like Christ by doing one thing—by following him in the overall style of life he chose for himself. . . . What activities did Jesus practice? Such things as solitude and silence, prayer, simple and sacrificial living, intense study, meditation upon God's Word and God's ways, and service to others.[6]

Willard's argument is that you will not be able to live like Christ if you are not doing the type of activities Christ did on a regular basis. The same is true with forgiving others. We will not be able to forgive others for Christ's sake and in his power if we are living a life void of the very lifestyle he embraced daily. Willard writes that the only reason a professional baseball player can hit a ninety-mile-an-hour fastball is because of the hours of practice in a batting cage, not the few swings during a game.[7] Forgiveness is not the type of activity you can dispense at a moment's notice without deep spiritual preparation. Hours spent meditating on the Scriptures, communing with God through solitude, fasting and a vibrant prayer life will all pave the way to making us receptive to forgiving others. The first step in forgiving our spouse must be taken well before the actual offense even occurs.

Second step: Embrace the pain. Forgiveness does not require that you minimize what has happened to you or that you pretend it didn't hurt. Paul tells us that when we encounter individuals who are in pain or who are mourning, we are not to tell them to tough it out, but to mourn with them (see Romans 12:15). If forgiveness entails releasing disappointment, anger or resentment toward your spouse, a necessary first step is to name and acknowledge those emotions. Smedes argues that forgiveness begins with the simplest of qualifications: we must bear our wounds. "Our wounds qualify us to forgive the way a broken leg qualifies us for entry to the emergency room. Forgiving is about healing wounds. So only people who bear the pain qualify for forgiving the person who inflicted it."[8]

Third step: Address disappointment with God. When our spouse apologizes for being irritable or late for dinner, forgiving her or him doesn't cause us to question God's faithfulness. When issues of trust or fidelity come into play, we may begin to question the goodness and provision of God. At marriage conferences and workshops, I've heard the heart cries of individuals whose faith has been shaken by the actions of an unfaithful or untrustworthy spouse: "How can God allow this to happen?" "I prayed my whole life for a soul mate, and this is what I get?" "Before we got engaged, I asked God over and over to confirm my decision. Why didn't he protect me?" Many times the spouses who are struggling feel guilty for even thinking such seemingly unspiritual thoughts. I tell them that God can handle their doubts and that they should read the raw emotions voiced by King David:

> Awake, O LORD! Why do you sleep? Rouse yourself! Do not reject us forever. Why do you hide your face and forget our misery and oppression? (Psalm 44:23-24)

> I am worn out calling for help; my throat is parched. My eyes fail, looking for my God. (69:3)

Why, O Lord, do you reject me and hide your face from
me? From my youth I have been afflicted and close to
death; I have suffered your terrors and am in despair. Your
wrath has swept over me; your terrors have destroyed me.
(88:14-16)

I pour out my complaint before him [the Lord]; before
him I tell my trouble. (142:2)

Eventually David's questioning does give way to trust, as re-
flected in Psalm 130:

O Lord, hear my voice. Let your ears be attentive to my
cry for mercy. If you, O Lord, kept a record of sins, O
Lord, who could stand? But with you there is forgiveness;
therefore you are feared. (vv. 2-4)[9]

If the offenses of your spouse have caused a rift between you
and God, it's best to get it out in the open. After all, an all-
knowing God already knows you have these doubts and powerful emotions, and it will help your communication climate with
him to acknowledge and verbalize them. It will also help your
climate with God to begin to formulate answers to troubling
questions, such as, Why would God allow my spouse to violate
my trust in him or her? Why didn't he do more to protect me
and my marriage?

While it's impossible to answer such probing questions in a
short amount of space, I find two thoughts comforting when
facing a crisis of faith. First, it is our ability to freely choose
good over evil that delights God. Sadly, in a fallen world, people
closest to us often make bad and hurtful choices. These bad
choices—and the pain they cause—are not God's fault. If he
interfered every time a person was about to hurt someone, he
would be stripping us of a key feature of what makes us human:
our freedom. Instead of forcing people to be good, God would

rather we choose to be kind and loving on our own. Theologian J. B. Phillips explains: "It is worth noting that the whole point of Christianity lies not in interference with the human power to choose, but in producing a willing consent to choose good rather than evil."[10]

Second, if you find yourself hurt by the actions of your spouse, know that you do not hurt alone—God hurts with you. In fact, God is not only aware of your pain but also knows first-hand what it feels like to be hurt by the actions of others. One of the central beliefs of our faith is that God put on human flesh and suffered many of the same evils that plague us. The prophet Isaiah informed his listeners that the coming Messiah would be a "man of sorrows, and familiar with suffering" (53:3). Even a casual reading of the Gospels shows that Isaiah's prophecy came true. In addition to physical affliction, Christ understands what it is like to have trust in others shattered and to be abandoned by those closest to him.[11]

Fourth step: Accept that forgiving your spouse is unconditional. This is the step in the process of forgiveness that we resist the most. After all, if our spouse doesn't ask for forgiveness or keeps on doing the same transgression over and over, she or he doesn't deserve to be forgiven, right? In a sense, no one deserves to be forgiven. Smedes explains:

> Forgiving is only for people who don't deserve it. Being sorry for the wrong we did does not earn us a right to be forgiven. How could it? There is no such thing as a right to be forgiven. Forgiving flows always and only from what theologians call grace—unearned, undeserved favor. Grace that is earned is not grace at all.[12]

Smedes is referring to the foundational Christian truth powerfully articulated by Paul: "For it is by grace you have been saved, through faith—and this not from yourselves, it is the gift of God" (Ephesians 2:8). The forgiveness you received from God through faith is a gift, and by definition, a gift cannot be earned. We graciously give our spouses the gift of forgiveness because that is what God offered to us.

However, forgiving your spouse doesn't mean that you stop being discerning. If your spouse has violated your trust by looking at pornography, you can forgive him or her and still discuss installing filters on the home computer. Forgiving your spouse for misusing credit cards and putting the family at financial risk doesn't mean that she or he can continue to have access to credit without firm accountability. As we will see in the next chapter, forgiving your spouse for verbal or physical abuse doesn't mean that he can continue to abuse. Our forgiveness is not conditional, but every marital climate must strive to create healthy conditions and set standards.

The unconditional nature of forgiveness is the most challenging, yet the most empowering. For Holocaust survivor Eva Kor, it has made all the difference. When she was ten years old, she and her sister were sent to Auschwitz concentration camp. There they were the victims of Dr. Josef Mengele's horrific experiments, resulting in lifelong medical problems for both of them, complications that would eventually contribute to her sister's death in 1993. What could Eva do with all the anger she had toward the Nazis and Mengele? At times, she felt the anger killing her from the inside. Her anger couldn't bring back her sister, but maybe forgiveness could heal her own spirit. After years of unrest, she decided to do the unthinkable in forgiving the now deceased Mengele and his descendants. She put her thoughts in a letter, which she read in Mengele's hometown.

To her surprise, Eva became the target of outraged Jews who couldn't believe that she could forgive monsters. "I've had people tell me forgiveness should come with pre-conditions. The person you're forgiving has to say he's sorry."[13]

For forgiveness to work, doesn't it need preconditions? For me to forgive, doesn't my spouse have to first admit he or she is sorry? And if my spouse never admits it, wouldn't it make a mockery of forgiveness for me to go ahead and forgive? Eva would say no. "The power to forgive can never be taken away from you. If you wait for the person who has wronged you to come to you and ask forgiveness, you are still at their mercy. You may be waiting for the rest of your life. That way, you will never be free. You will always be the victim."[14]

For our marital climate to be healthy and thriving, we must diligently acknowledge each other, foster trust, communicate expectations and be committed to each other. Yet let us never forget the simple advice of an aging philosopher to his children: if a couple is determined and willing to forgive, there isn't anything they can't overcome. The rest, it turns out, is merely nuts and bolts.

THINK IT OVER

1. Cicero described crucifixion as "a most cruel and disgusting punishment," yet Christ willingly endured it to forgive you of your sins. How does this act of divine humility change how you view forgiveness in general, and forgiving your spouse in particular?

2. Dallas Willard makes the point that to live and forgive like Christ, we must adopt his overall lifestyle and practice daily disciplines such as solitude and silence, prayer, simple and sacrificial living, and intense study and meditation on God's Word. What keeps you from adopting this lifestyle on a daily basis? What practical changes do you need to make to your schedule or habits to be more Christlike?

3. Have you ever experienced or known anyone who has expe-

rienced disappointment with God due to the transgression
of a loved one toward her or him? In the midst of our disappointment, why is it sometimes hard to be honest with God
and voice our feelings?

4. Do you agree or disagree with those who opposed Eva Kor—
the woman who forgave Josef Mengele—and claimed that
forgiveness must come with preconditions and that a person
must first ask to be forgiven? Specifically, in order for you to
forgive, does your spouse have to first admit he or she is
sorry?

Hurricane Warnings

When Conflict Turns to Abuse

You start lying to yourself the minute the physical wounds go away," a somber Rihanna told the media concerning her beating at the hands of ex-boyfriend Chris Brown.[1] In 2009 the media were saturated with leaked police photos of the battered pop star. She told police that Brown put her in a headlock twice, punched her and bit her ears and fingers. Abuse is not new to Rihanna, because she grew up watching her father physically abusing her mother and swore she would never stay in an abusive relationship, but did for a time with Brown. She decided to tell her story because abused women often hide out of embarrassment. Tragically, Rihanna's and her mother's predicaments are all too common. Consider these unsettling facts:

- Battery is the single largest cause of injury to women—more frequent than auto accidents, muggings and rapes combined.

- Women in the United States are in nine times more physical danger in their own homes than they are on the street.

- Fifteen to 25 percent of all battered women are pregnant.
- Men commit 90 to 95 percent of all domestic violence assaults.
- Only 9 percent of women who suffer from assault by their partner call the police. In addition, only 8 percent of abused women press charges against their partner, and 72 percent of this small percentage drop their charges.
- Twenty-five percent of women and 30 percent of men regard violence as a normal and even positive part of marriage.
- Twenty percent of girls between ages of 14 and 18 reported being hit, slapped, shoved or raped by a date.[2]

For many women, the climate within their marriage or relationships is frightening and dangerous. In the past three chapters, I argued that conflict is inevitable to all marriages and if handled properly can be constructive to a marriage's overall climate. What the women described in these statistics experience is not conflict but abuse. There is a big difference between storms that occasionally challenge a couple's climate and communication or actions that are abusive and dangerous.

The first step in confronting verbal, emotional and/or physical abuse is to recognize the different forms abuse can take. We'll also consider what communication scholars identify as the *cycle of abuse*. Finally, what should a woman do if she suspects she's caught up in the cycle of abuse with her intimate partner?[3]

Before identifying the different forms of abuse, let's consider the violent world women experienced during the time of Jesus and how he and his followers reacted to it.

Women in first-century Palestine had no credibility or voice in a male-dominated culture. Many first-century rabbis taught that it was better to burn the law than to teach it to a woman.

One famous saying stated, "Blessed is he whose children are male, but woe to him whose children are female." In many parts of the Roman Empire, girls received little or no education and were married at puberty and often before. Under Roman law, a woman was considered a child, regardless of her age, and would live her entire life under the authority of a man. Once married, a husband could secure a divorce by simply commanding her to leave the house, forcing her into a life of poverty or prostitution. This constant threat of divorce served as a powerful type of emotional abuse used by the husband to control the wife. Trapped inside the home, she lived with the knowledge that under Roman law her husband could beat her if it was deemed necessary for discipline or her personal moral development. Her life was filled with fear, low self-esteem and danger.

Jesus shattered social norms and taboos surrounding how men treated women in Roman times by interacting with women, showing care and respect regardless of their social status. When he healed women, he gently touched them and allowed them to touch him (see Matthew 9:18-26; Luke 13:10-16). He took time to speak at length to a shunned Samaritan woman at a well (see John 4) and to a lowly Canaanite woman (see Matthew 15:21-28). Two women, Mary and Martha, are considered his closest friends.

Christ's followers continued to promote respect and concern for women and to give clear instructions to a Christian husband. Paul specifically exhorts husbands to "love your wives, just as Christ loved the church and gave himself up for her" (Ephesians 5:25). Similarly, husbands are to "love their wives as their own bodies" (v. 28). Paul argues that, just as ridiculous as it would be for a man to hate and abuse his physical body, it is absurd to hate and harm a wife who has become "one flesh" with him (Genesis 2:23-24). Peter tells husbands that they are obligated to be considerate and respectful to their wife and mindful that, as a physically "weaker partner," they are vulnerable to physical abuse (1 Peter 3:7). He warns husbands that if they fail to treat their wives in an honorable way, their prayers will be hindered and their relationship with God marred. In a moving paraphrase of Paul's words, Eugene Peterson sums up Scripture's charge to men as they seek to love their wives in a way that honors Christ:

> Husbands, go all out in your love for your wives, exactly as Christ did for the church—a love marked by giving, not getting. Christ's love makes the church whole. His words evoke her beauty. Everything he does and says is designed to bring the best out of her, dressing her in dazzling white silk, radiant with holiness. And that is how husbands ought to love their wives. They're really doing themselves a favor—since they're already "one" in marriage. No one abuses his own body, does he? No, he feeds and pampers it. That's how Christ treats us, the church, since we are part of his body. . . . And this provides a good picture of how each husband is to treat his wife, loving himself in loving her, and how each wife is to honor her husband. (Ephesians 5:25-30, 33 *The Message*)

Considering the imbalanced and often abusive power relationship between husbands and wives in the Greco-Roman world, Paul's and Peter's admonishments to husbands to be faithful, sacrificial, respectful and nonabusive toward their wives can be seen as a powerful call to confront abuse in a culture where women were physically and emotionally at risk.

Just as Christ and his followers sought to confront abuse in their day, we are called by Christ to do the same. The first step in confronting abuse is recognizing the different forms abuse can take in a harmful communication climate: physical, verbal and emotional.

PHYSICAL ABUSE

Physical abuse is the intentional infliction of physical pain, injury or discomfort through, for example, hitting, slapping, pushing, kicking, biting, pulling hair, tackling or holding a person down. Physical abuse is *any* contact intended to cause physical harm or discomfort.

One day, while living in North Carolina, I was surprised to see a police car pull up into my neighbor's driveway and even more surprised to see my neighbor being led out by police in handcuffs. When we went over to talk to his wife, she showed us three scratch marks where her husband had grabbed her arm during an argument. When one of the police officers noticed the marks, he was required by law to arrest her husband.

One of the myths surrounding abuse is that women are partially to blame for their husband's violent actions, that they drive men to abuse. Nothing could be further from the truth. There is simply no excuse for a man to touch a woman in anger, ever. While I didn't witness the argument between my neighbors that prompted a call to the police, I do know the husband had no right to touch her in anger. When he did, the trust between them was shattered, and the police acted in accordance with what Paul tells us the state was designed by God to do: stop evil (see Romans 13:3).

VERBAL ABUSE

Verbal abuse consists of "words that attack or injure, that cause one to believe the false, or that speak falsely of one, " according to Patricia Evans.[4] Evans is a communication specialist who wrote the landmark book *The Verbally Abusive Relationship* and has spent her career studying the devastating effects of verbal, emotional and psychological abuse. In her early work she interviewed forty verbally abused women from age twenty-one to sixty-six and identified key characteristics of verbal abuse.

First, *verbal abuse is emotionally and psychologically hurtful.* The counselors I interviewed while writing this chapter told me that verbal abuse is in some ways more damaging than physical abuse. Over time a verbally abused person's sense of self is deeply damaged, her confidence is destroyed, and the abused begins to question her sanity.

The Scriptures speak of the power our words have in affecting another person. In Proverbs "reckless words" are presented as a piercing sword (see 12:17), a deceitful tongue that can crush a person's spirit (see 15:4) and a word spoken in the wrong way that can "break a bone" (25:15). James cautions that the tongue can be a "world of evil" and compares it to a "fire" that can set ablaze an entire forest by one spark or utterance (3:5-6).

Two years ago, my two oldest boys' high school was hit by a California wildfire. One building was lost, and the trees and landscape surrounding the school were consumed by flames and charred. To this day, you can see the damage the fire caused to the surroundings—a powerful reminder of the intense heat. Our words are equally powerful and can render psychological and emotional damage that takes years to recover from, if recovery ever happens. One Old Testament scholar notes, "That awesome power of life and death that resides in the tongue makes it literally a lethal weapon—to others and ourselves."[5]

Second, *verbal abuse attacks the vulnerabilities and abilities of the partner.* Over time, the abused spouse starts to think that *she* is the problem. Devoid of any encouragement, the abused questions her abilities, talents or strengths. One woman Evans interviewed commented, "I heard so often that I was a lousy driver, I really began to think I had a problem driving. I think I was brainwashed."[6] In considering relational trust, it's reasonable to expect that not only would our spouse be there for us in difficult times but also would he be our advocate and supporter.

An abused spouse goes through marriage with little or no verbal support or encouragement, only criticism.

Finally, *verbal abuse may be overt or covert.* Overt abuse can take the form of angry outbursts or name-calling. All of us have raised our voice in the heat of an argument, but verbal abusers use angry outbursts to intimidate and strike fear into a spouse. An abused spouse walks on eggshells, never knowing what will set her spouse into a verbal rage. While a proverb wisely counsels to not "associate with one easily angered" (22:24), an abused spouse has no choice; she is trapped.

Name-calling strikes at the heart of the abused spouse's insecurities. As a former detective and the author of a book on domestic violence, Donald Stewart vividly describes the hurt caused by name-calling. He writes,

> If she's struggling with something in her physical appearance, he may call her fat or ugly. If she didn't finish high school, he may call her stupid, ignorant, or a dropout, etc. If she's been laid off from a job or didn't get a promotion, she may hear herself being described as a loser. Most important to remember is that most verbal abuse has no basis in fact—thin women are often told they are fat, and smart women are told they are stupid.[7]

Covert verbal abuse is hidden aggression that undermines the confidence of the abused. Evans identified *countering* as perhaps the most destructive form of covert abuse; the abuser consistently counters or disagrees with the thoughts, perceptions and experiences of the abused. One woman described her experience:

> If I say anything directly or express my thoughts on something, Curt says it's the opposite. I feel like I can't say anything without it being put down. I don't think there's any-

thing I can say that he won't counter. What he's really saying is, "No, that's not the way it is," even about my most personal experience of something.[8]

One of the key characteristics of a healthy communication climate is our ability and willingness to acknowledge the perspective of our spouse. Countering is the intentional attempt to injure another by refusing to acknowledge his or her perspective.

EMOTIONAL ABUSE

When people think of emotional abuse, they sometimes think of two people being mean to each other or overly critical. However, emotional abuse is much more than that, and it can create deep emotional and psychological scars. Emotional abuse is defined as any "nonphysical behavior that is designed to control, intimidate, subjugate, demean, punish, or isolate another person through the use of degradation, humiliation, or fear."[9] While emotional abuse shares many characteristics with verbal abuse—judging, accusing, discounting, humiliation, berating—and the same results for the abused—loss of self-worth and self-confidence—there are two characteristics unique to emotional abuse.

First, while emotional abuse primarily consists of nonphysical behaviors, there is a physical component to emotional abuse called *symbolic violence.* Symbolic violence entails showing displeasure toward a spouse by slamming doors, throwing objects or driving recklessly when the spouse is in the car. It can also manifest itself through destroying or threatening to destroy objects that have great personal value to the abused spouse, such as diaries, family photos, jewelry or gifts from children.

Unique to emotional abuse is also the use of the "silent treatment" to isolate or punish a spouse. Counselors will often note that the opposite of love is not hate, but indifference. The reaction of anger or hate is at least a reaction, while silence is the refusal to acknowledge a person's existence. Philosopher William James argued that the greatest punishment he could think of would be to exist in a community and have no one acknowledge you or interact with you. An abuser inflicts deep emotional pain when he refuses to interact with his spouse in order to punish her.

Before we consider how these different forms of abuse manifest themselves in the cycle of abuse, it's important to understand that often all three forms are present in an abusive relationship. Seldom is an abuser merely verbally abusive without emotional or physical abuse also occurring. As researchers have studied abuse and interacted with women who have come out of abusive relationships, they have identified a common pattern that you may be experiencing, or you may know of someone who has described a similar pattern. The name counselors and researchers have given this pattern is the *cycle of abuse.*

THE CYCLE OF ABUSE

I first became aware that there was a cycle to relational abuse when I was single and living in Ohio. My roommate and I lived beneath an engaged couple in an apartment complex, and they occasionally had loud, intense arguments. One day, in the midst of one of their arguments, we heard someone crash into a wall and then the sound of a woman moaning. We immediately called 911 and waited for the police. When the police arrived they asked, "Ma'am, what happened to your lip, and why is it bleeding?" She explained to the officer that she had fallen. "Are you sure?" the officer asked. When she assured them she had just tripped, they told them to keep it down, and left. My roommate and I were dumbfounded. Why didn't she tell the police what had happened?

The next day we expected to see her car packed and her moving out. What happened next shocked us. We could hear laughing coming from their apartment, and later that evening the couple walked hand in hand to his car and drove away. He treated her like a queen in the weeks immediately following the incident, and they didn't fight much at all for the next several months. Then slowly the arguments started again.

Sound familiar? Counselors note that for many couples whose climate is marked by abuse, the abuse follows a cyclical pattern marked by four stages.

Stage one: Tension. In this stage, the batterer feels tension at work or home and starts to feel frustrated, insecure or angry. As the tension mounts, the abuse escalates in the form of threats, shouting, insults, taunts, name-calling, destroying of valuables and so on. In chronically abusive relationships, the abused picks up on the mounting tension and tries to make sure she and the children walk on eggshells in the home to keep the abuser from becoming increasingly agitated or violent.

Stage two: Explosion. Frustration and tension erupt into physical abuse. The abuser throws a spouse against a wall, grabs her by the hair, kicks her, punches her, cuts her or slaps her. Often this stage ends with a spouse requiring medical attention. In some situations, this stage can even tragically end in the death of a spouse.

Stage three: Remorse. The abuser comes to the abused spouse and is deeply apologetic. He acts remorseful and contrite, and he promises it will never happen again. Abused women report seeing in this stage the "good person" inside the abuser, the person they fell in love with and married. During this stage, the battered spouse will come to see the abuse as an aberration and the contrite man as the real man.

Stage four: Honeymoon. The batterer dates his spouse all over again. He acts lovingly toward her and seeks to meet her emotional and physical needs. The abused spouse becomes convinced that the physical act of violence will not happen again—even if it has happened regularly in the marriage. Slowly tension begins to build in the life of the abuser, and the cycle begins again.

HOW TO RESPOND

If you have even the slightest inkling that you are caught in the cycle of abuse, don't ignore your suspicions.

First, resist the tendency to move toward denial. If your husband exhibits some of the traits of physical, verbal or emotional abuse described in this chapter, you must be open to the possibility that abuse may be occurring. For many women, the thought that they are being abused is a scary and deeply discouraging possibility. With all our expectations of marriage, most never in their wildest dreams thought abuse would be a possibility. Some women think that their husband's name-calling or punching is just a phase or rough patch he is going through or that his angry outbursts will stop if she became a better wife. Yet, what if he doesn't stop? What if this is a cycle of abuse that will only continue to grow more and more violent?

Even more disturbing to think about is if you have children who are part of an abusive climate. How is it influencing your children to watch this abuse? What is the message you are sending them? It is from our parents that we learn what is and is not acceptable in relating to other people. If abuse is happening, you are conditioning your daughter to accept and commit to a man who may also abuse her physically, emotionally and verbally. If abuse is happening and you do nothing, you are telling your son that it is okay for a man to treat a woman the way your husband treats you. Eighty-five percent of male batterers report witnessing domestic violence in their own homes growing up.[10] If you have even the slightest suspicion of abuse happening in your marriage, don't ignore it.

Second, talk it through with someone you trust. Find a person who will listen to you, refrain from judging you and help you process. Women who are being abused need to realize that they are being deeply affected, often without knowing it, in an abusive relationship. One woman trapped in the cycle of abuse would hurry along the explosion stage before the holidays, ensuring that her husband would be in the honeymoon stage when relatives came to visit. Trapped in the abuse, she had learned to work the cycle to promote harmony for the holidays.

Finding someone to help obtain an objective picture of your marriage is crucial. If possible financially, a Christian counselor is ideal. Many Christian counselors are trained to catch the tell-tale signs of abuse and can help you develop a plan individually and as a couple. If a Christian counselor is too expensive, check into pastoral counseling through your church. If you are afraid that the pastors of your church will not believe you or will minimize your fears, go to another church and ask to meet with a pastor to discuss your situation confidentially.

Third, become informed. If you are becoming convinced that abuse is happening in your marriage, you need to equip yourself with information. There are many websites that offer useful information, resources and contact numbers. For example, the National Coalition Against Domestic Violence site (www.ncadv.org) and FamilyLife (www.Familylife.com) offer important information on marital abuse. A computer is also the easiest and quickest way to obtain the phone number of a local shelter or abuse hotline. The staff at an abuse hotline can provide everything from advice to a listening ear to a safe place to go. However, make sure that the computer you are using is not easily accessible by your abuser, who could become angry that you are seeking to empower yourself. Most libraries have computers and printers that are easily accessi-

ble. While at the library, you can also check out—in addition
to the Evans and Stewart books mentioned in this chapter—
two powerful resources written by Nancy Nason-Clark and
Catherine Kroeger: *No Place for Abuse* and *Refuge from Abuse*
(InterVarsity Press).

Fourth, do not let fear paralyze you. Many women do not
leave an abusive situation or call 911[11] when abuse is happening
because of paralyzing questions: What will I do if he gets ar-
rested? Will he lose his job? How will I make it financially?
What will happen to the kids? Who will pay legal fees if I go to
court? What happens when he gets out of jail? What will my
family or friends think? Will I lose the house? Who will take
care of us? If a woman starts to suspect that abuse is occurring,
it will be crucial for her to turn to God and give her fears to
him. Any woman thinking about confronting her spouse's
abuse or leaving an abusive situation will need to trust God to
take care of her and her family.

Taking care of her children is a real concern for a woman
thinking about leaving an abusive situation. Jesus tackled these
concerns directly when he told his followers, "Do not worry
about your life, what you will eat or drink; or about your body,
what you will wear. Is not life more important than food, and
the body more important than clothes?" (Matthew 6:25). Jesus
is using a teaching technique here called "the principle of the
greater to the lesser." If God gave you the miracle of life (the
greater), he'll certainly provide you with food (the lesser) to
sustain it. Likewise, if God gave you a complex and wonderful
body (the greater), he'll most certainly give you clothes (the
lesser) to cover and protect it.

As we'll read in the next chapter, this life he gave you and
your children is the same life Jesus died for on the cross. For
the apostle Paul, the death of Jesus was the greatest example of
the principle of the greater to the lesser. He writes, "He who did

not spare his own Son, but gave him up for us all [greater]—how will he not also, along with him, graciously give us all things [lesser]?" (Romans 8:32).

Do you see what Paul is saying? If God gave you and your children Jesus, which is the greatest possible thing he could give, you can be assured he will provide for you *all* the lesser things (a place to stay, food, clothes, money) if you decide to leave an abusive situation. Because God is committed to caring for us and our daily needs, Jesus tells us, "Do not worry about tomorrow" (Matthew 6:34). The decision to talk to another person about abuse will be scary and will produce many anxious questions and doubts. Yet the same God who graciously gave you life will also guide you and provide for you.

■ ■ ■

Vera's husband slapped her hard across the face for waking him up for work before his ride had arrived.[12] She ran to the bedroom and locked the door. Crumbling to the floor, she cried out to God for help. To her surprise, she heard a still small voice: "Are you serious?" She knew it was God responding to her. "Yes. I can't take this anymore. I'm done." What the Lord asked her to do next changed the course of her life. She felt God give her the strength to reach out to her sister, who encouraged her to call a domestic violence shelter. It was one of the hardest and scariest calls she'd ever made.

In talking to the woman who answered the phone, Vera explained that she and her infant son were in trouble, but did not mention acts of domestic violence for fear of getting her husband in trouble. The woman was compassionate, but told her the center couldn't help because it only worked with abused women. Distraught, Vera called her sister and told her she couldn't bring herself to "out" her husband. "Vera," her sister said, "call back and tell the truth." When she did, the center said she should come in for an interview.

With her mom, Vera went back to her apartment to quickly pack some things while her husband was at work. Waiting for her was some money and a note that told her how sorry he was, how much he wanted "us" to work and that he loved her. She hesitated for a moment, then crumbled the note and stuffed the money in her pocket.

Vera has never looked back. The center surrounded her with friends who had been there, helped her get legal advice and a job, and even made it possible for her to complete her education. Vera came to see each step of faith she took and every person who helped her as being an intricate part of God's plan to provide for her and her son. "The day I left him was the beginning of my new life."

THINK IT OVER

1. In chapter one, we considered the question "Who's in the room with you?" In your parents' or other relatives' relationships, were there any signs of physical, verbal or emotional abuse between them that may influence how you view what's appropriate in conflict or how you interact with your spouse?

2. In the beginning of the chapter, it was stated that 25 percent of women and 30 percent of men regard violence as a normal and even positive part of marriage. Where do you think couples get that idea? How can we shield ourselves (and our children) from harmful cultural messages?

3. Have you and your husband ever had an argument that you think may have exhibited traits of physical, verbal or emotional abuse? Do you think you and your spouse have fallen into the cycle of abuse? What prompts the cycle to occur?

4. If you suspected abuse was happening in your marriage,

what would keep you from talking to someone about it? Embarrassment? The possibility of him finding out? Fear that people will not take you seriously? Fear of the unknown?

5. Former detective and author Donald Stewart challenges men to ask their wives three questions:[13]

   • Are you or the children afraid of me?

   • Do you feel safe enough to tell me how you feel about the relationship?

   • Am I controlling you or suffocating you with my demands and expectations?

Our Communication Climate with God
and Why It Means Everything

Human beings can't make one another really happy for long.
You cannot love a fellow creature fully till you love God.

C. S. LEWIS, *THE GREAT DIVORCE*

*T*he most important truth about communication climates doesn't come from an expert in communication or a marriage counselor. It comes from a man who spent a lifetime considering how our relationship with God influences all aspects of our lives. In his writings, C. S. Lewis provides an insight into what we've been discussing in *Marriage Forecasting* that warrants our focus as we end this book: "You cannot love a fellow creature fully till you love God."

Just as there is a communication climate between you and your spouse, there also exists a communication climate between you and God. In fact, we were created to experience a relationship with God marked by a climate of acknowledgment, trust, commitment and expectations. Unfortunately, when sin entered the world, our relationship with God was shattered, and we turned from him to human relationships as our primary means of intimacy. Tragically, we traded a perfect relational climate for an imperfect one. We retain the desire for divine acknowledgment, trust and commitment, but turn to fallen spouses and family members to provide it for us. Lewis accurately predicts the folly of this strategy: "Human beings can't make one another really happy for long."

What does Lewis suggest we do? "When I have learnt to love God better than my earthly dearest I shall love my earthly dearest better than I do now."[1] Why? By allowing myself to be loved by a perfect God who does not have mood swings or bad days, my need for transcendent love is fulfilled. Being loved by the divine lover within a stable, healthy communication climate frees me to be content with human love communicated in an often unstable, inconsistent climate.

The most important step we can take in improving our communication climate with our spouse is to first focus on our climate with God. If our relational climate with God is lacking, we'll turn our unsatisfied hearts to our spouse and ask her or him to compensate. In this chapter we'll explore what the Scriptures state our climate with God should be like and then take a reading of our climate with God to determine how our experience matches that description. In considering our relationship with God, we'll start with trust. Just as in human relationships, trust is the foundational issue that influences all others aspects of a relational climate with God.

TRUST

When it comes to God, two important questions come into play: First, is God trustworthy? Second, will God come through for *me*?

Is God trustworthy? The Scriptures affirm that all of God's words are true and that his faithfulness "reaches to the skies" (Psalm 57:10). To say that God is faithful "means that God will always do what he has said and fulfill what he has promised," says theologian Wayne Grudem.[2] This means that God can always be counted on and trusted. "Indeed, the essence of true faith is taking God at his word and relying on him to do as he has promised."[3]

All of us have experienced the disappointment brought about by a spouse failing to follow through on a promise. Sometimes this broken promise is brought about by carelessness or immaturity, and sometimes it's brought on by a character defect. Yet God's promises are always fulfilled, because there are no character defects with God.

In addition to being trustworthy and faithful, God is holy. Comprehending the holiness of God had a profound effect on one of Israel's most revered prophets. When Israel's king dies and the prophet Isaiah goes into the temple to meet with God, he is awestruck. Circling God are angels, called seraphim, who continually call out, "Holy, holy, holy" (Isaiah 6:3). The sole purpose of these angels is to draw Isaiah's (and our) attention to the fact that God is holy and thus is completely and utterly separated from sin and evil. Not only is it impossible for God to sin, he is not even *tempted* to do what is wrong. When it comes to self-trust, God not only meets the highest of standards but sets the standard. Yet, what is the level of relational trust that exists between you and God?

Relational trust entails confidence in others to be reliable. Though it may seem odd, it's important to reflect on how much confidence you have in the reliability of God. It's one thing to believe that the Scriptures teach that God is trustworthy, faithful and holy, and another to embrace those truths personally. Sometimes we face deep struggles that cause us to question whether we can trust God to be there in times of hurt or desperation.

Lewis went through a period when he deeply questioned the reliability of God. When his wife, Joy, died of cancer, he was devastated. In *A Grief Observed* he lets us in on his questioning: "Where is God? . . . Go to Him when your need is desperate, when all other help is in vain, and what do you find? A door slammed in your face and a sound of bolting and double bolting on the inside. After that, silence. You may as well turn away."[4] Can you relate? Have there been times in your life or marriage when you've relied on God and he seemed not to hold up his end of the deal? You prayed you'd be spared from layoffs, and you were the first to receive a pink slip. You gathered the family together to pray for the biopsy test results, and they came back positive. You felt God lead you to take a step of faith and start a business, and the bottom fell out of the economy. You prayed for your daughter's faith to flourish, and now she's in college and doesn't want anything to do with church. You prayed for your kids' transition to the new school, and they still don't have any close friends. With each unanswered prayer, your relational trust with God seems to weaken.

One of my dearest friends unexpectedly lost his dream job and spent two years searching for work. During that time, his family faced severe financial stress that took its toll physically and emotionally on him and his marriage. I prayed daily for him. I can't tell you how many times he'd make it through the interview process and be one of two candidates for a job that seemed perfect for him and would allow him to pay all his debts, only to have the company go with the other candidate. After a while, what do you say? After a while, how do you find enough trust or faith to pray one more time?

Watching him go through those difficult times—exasperated by seemingly unanswered prayers—made me question my

trust level with God. If my family hit tough financial challenges, would God be there for us? Would our prayers for help
be met with the same unsettling silence my friend or Lewis
experienced? The pause I felt in my spirit was unsettling and
sent a chill through my own relational climate with God.

In his book *Disappointment with God*, Philip Yancey notes
that disappointment with God does not come only with dramatic events like the death of a loved one or the loss of job, but
in the culmination of small disappointments. "I have found
that petty disappointments tend to accumulate over time, un-
dermining my faith with a lava flow of doubt. I start to wonder
whether God cares about everyday details—about me," Yancey
writes.[5] I remember one week in which I received two rejection
letters for articles I had sent off for publication. It wasn't like
one of my children had a lingering illness or my wife had been
in a traffic accident and God hadn't answered my prayers for
healing or protection. Yet I had worked hard on those articles,
and I was sad to see them turned down. Did God care? Is he
attentive to the desires of an aspiring writer? Does God concern
himself with our goals and dreams?

If we come to doubt whether we can trust God, we sometimes
expect our spouse to pick up the slack. We trust him or her to
provide what only God can provide, thus setting our spouse up
for failure and sending a chill through our marital climate.

ACKNOWLEDGMENT

A key part of acknowledgment is being mindful and attentive
toward a person. One of the amazing truths of Scripture is that
the God of the universe is attentive to us. First, he is aware of
and acknowledges our individual presence. Jesus taught that
not even a sparrow falls to the ground without God taking notice. If sparrows warrant God's attention, how much more do
individuals made in his image? "The very hairs of your head are

all numbered," Jesus assured his listeners (Mathew 10:30).

One man who understood God's mindfulness toward him was King David. In one of his writings, David proclaims, "You know when I sit and when I rise. . . . You discern my going out and my lying down; you are familiar with all my ways" (Psalm 139:2-3). David even wracks his brain with hypothetical scenarios: "Where can I go from your Spirit? Where can I flee from your presence? If I go up to the heavens, you are there; if I make my bed in the depths, you are there. If I rise on the wings of the dawn, if I settle on the far side of the sea, even there your hand will guide me" (vv. 7-10). In every situation, David can imagine God is (and will be) there acknowledging him.

Second, the Scriptures teach that God acknowledges and is attentive to our prayers. David believes not only that God is mindful of him but also that God listens and responds to him. A confident David writes, "O LORD, I call to you; come quickly to me. Hear my voice when I call to you. May my prayer be set before you like incense" (Psalm 141:1-2). Last year I spent two weeks in New Delhi, India, on a research project. Part of that project entailed going into Hindu temples, where worshipers bang on tin gongs to awaken and gain the attention of the local gods. In contrast, Christians do not believe they have to rouse a slumbering God, but pray to one whose "ears are attentive to their prayer" (1 Peter 3:12).

The most significant way God acknowledges us is in the fact that Christ died for us as individuals. The main point of the parable of the lost coin, the lost sheep and the prodigal son is that God went looking for *the one*. A woman loses a coin and turns her house upside down looking for it; a shepherd leaves his flock in open country to pursue the one lost sheep; a father leaves his community, servants and family and runs toward his wayward son (Luke 15:1-31). Christian author and philosopher Peter Kreeft draws this conclusion:

He didn't do that [died on the cross] for "dear occupant," he did it for you. . . . He didn't die for humanity. Humanity is an idea, an abstraction, a concept. Fools and politicians talk about dying for concepts; actual soldiers die for their buddies. Humanity doesn't exist. You do. The nail prints in His hands spell out your name.[6]

God makes it clear that this relationship with him is permanent and his commitment to us unwavering.

COMMITMENT

If commitment is lacking in a relationship, the marital climate cannot help but be unstable. Commitment is both the assumption of a future together and the willingness to invest in the relationship. The Scriptures make it clear that our relationship with God is stable and our future secure. The writer of Hebrews records God's promise to believers everywhere: "Never will I leave you; never will I forsake you" (13:5). After commissioning his disciples and future believers to take the gospel to all nations, Jesus tells them (and us) that regardless of the difficulties they'll encounter, he'll be with them "always, to the very end of the age" (Matthew 28:20). Paul doesn't mince words when he tells the persecuted church that at times they'll feel like sheep being prepared for slaughter, yet in spite of their suffering, they are still "more than conquerors" (Romans 8:37). Why? Because of the assurance that "neither angels nor demons, neither the present nor the future, nor any powers" can separate them from "the love of God" (vv. 38-39).

These early believers could be assured that God was committed to them because God had given them a symbol of his unending commitment. Much like a husband and wife giving each other rings on their wedding day to signify their love, God gave believers a sign of his love and commitment—Christ. "If

God is for us, who can be against us?" Paul powerfully wrote to
the believers in Rome. "He who did not spare his own Son, but
gave him up for us all" (Romans 8:31-32). Today, in a world of
starter marriages and no-fault divorce, it's comforting to know
that our relational climate with God is built on an unwavering
commitment rooted in the trustworthiness of God and symbolized in the sacrificial death of Christ.

Another facet of commitment is the willingness to invest in
a relationship. God is committed to invest in our lives to help
us flourish as individuals. Paul states that each one of us who
is a follower of Christ is "God's workmanship, created in Christ
Jesus to do good works" (Ephesians 2:10). It is from the Greek
word *poiema* (workmanship) that we get the word "poem." It is
said that the poet Langston Hughes would sometimes be so in-
vested in his literary works that he would write only one word
a day. His poems meant so much to him that he'd spend hours,
even days, selecting a single word to add to a poem that would
eventually endure the test of time. The same is true with God
in his handling of us. God is committed to conforming us into
the image of his Son. We can be assured that "he who began a
good work in you will carry it on to completion until the day of
Christ Jesus" (Philippians 1:6).

While we have such strong assurances from God that our future
with him is secure, we still can have moments when we doubt his
commitment and question whether he is investing in the relationship. King David, so mindful of God's acknowledgment of him,
still struggled through periods of questioning God's commitment
to him. With powerful emotion he wrote, "My God, my God, why
have you forsaken me? Why are you so far from saving me, so far
from the words of my groaning?" (Psalm 22:1). Ironically, the same
David that had laid his prayers before God like sweet-smelling incense earlier in the psalm laments that God is silent: "O my God,
I cry out by day, but you do not answer" (v. 2).

It's difficult to feel like you are God's workmanship when you feel forsaken and your prayers are going unanswered. Ancient theologians, such as St. John of the Cross, referred to feelings of abandonment by God as dark nights of the soul. A dark night of the soul is a period of time where God removes all signs of his presence from a believer. Why would God do that? John Coe, a theologian who considers a dark night of the soul from a psychological perspective, suggests that God wants his followers to judge his commitment not by fluctuating feelings but by trust. Coe writes: "However, God is deeply committed to helping [Christians] re-focus, to see that a feeling is not the proper measure of his presence, and to see that he has been and will be the only true difference." At times, we will *feel* God is not close to us or responding to us. God's desire is that his followers "trust him by faith, even in darkness, rather than in themselves and their senses."[7] While in the midst of a dark night of the soul, we can easily think that God is no longer committed to us or has stopped investing in the relationship, and in such moments, we may turn to our spouse and seek a level of commitment or investment only possible through God.

EXPECTATIONS

On the day you started a relationship with God, expectations formed. Words and phrases like *Savior, heavenly Father, personal relationship with Jesus, power of the Holy Spirit, peace of Christ, prayer, Spirit's guiding, God's will, joy of the Lord, conviction of the Spirit, still small voice* became part of your vocabulary and shaped your expectations. How these phrases were defined and expressed were greatly influenced by the type of church or faith community you joined. Regardless of our community, we all long to know God in an authentic way. In his book *Knowing the Face of God*, Tim Stafford writes,

We hunger to know God personally, not merely to talk about him but to experience him as a living character. He is our father; we long to feel his arms. He has broken down all barriers to love us; we hunger to be in his possession. This hope drives us on, and it also frustrates us because we get only glimmers, nothing solid.[8]

What are your expectations when you come to God? When you open the Bible? When you pray? Do you expect to get only a glimmer of God or to encounter something more solid? I have a friend who, when she prays, is often moved to tears and regularly receives strong impressions from the Lord that she passes on to others. I've not had those experiences, and I've often been envious of her intimacy with God. When it comes to God, how do we determine what are realistic or unrealistic expectations? Is it realistic to expect to have regular tear-filled times of prayer? Should I expect or seek strong impressions from the Lord concerning my spouse or friends, and should I be disappointed if I don't receive them?

When I first became a Christian, I was told that I was entering a "personal relationship" with God, a relationship that would be the most intimate I would ever experience. Yet, if I'm honest, sometimes my relationship with God is flat and often unreal. Sometimes while praying, I feel that I'm just talking to myself. What should I expect during times of prayer and while reading the Scriptures?

Just as I need to come up with a list of evolving expectations with my spouse, I need to come up with a similar list with God—a list of constitutive rules concerning what counts as prayer, worship, intimacy, Spirit's guiding and so on. If our expectations—spoken and unspoken—continually go unmet, we will move away from God and put more pressure on our spouse to meet needs only God can satisfy.

So, where are you with God? What is your climate like with God at this moment? It's time to take a reading of the climate between you and God. Just as in taking a reading of your marital climate, these questions will first ask you to assign a number value (one being the lowest and five being the highest) and then ask a follow-up question that allows you to write down thoughts and dig a little deeper.

Trust
Overall, I feel I can trust God.

    1   2   3   4   5

Consider: What has God done in my life to make it easy for me to trust him?

I trust that God is looking out for my welfare and the welfare of my spouse.

    1   2   3   4   5

Consider: Are there any struggles I have faced that make me feel less convinced that God is reliable?

In the past two years, I'm disappointed in how God has rewarded my trust in him.

    1   2   3   4   5

Consider: Is my trust more swayed by significant events or by the accumulation of small disappointments?

Acknowledgment
Overall, I feel acknowledged by God.

    1   2   3   4   5

Consider: When interacting with God do I view myself as unique (I-Thou) or merely as one of his many followers (I-You)?

When going through my day, do I have the sense that God is with me or watching over me?

1   2   3   4   5

Consider: What can I do to facilitate a sense that God is with me in the car, office or grocery store?

I believe that Jesus suffered and died to secure *my* salvation.

1   2   3   4   5

Consider: What keeps me from fully embracing the fact that "the nail prints in His hands spell out your name," as Peter Kreeft wrote? Does it seem egotistical? Unbiblical?

Commitment
Overall, I believe God is utterly committed to me.

1   2   3   4   5

Consider: Is there any situation or sin that would cause God to abandon me?

I believe God's greatest symbol of commitment is Christ's death for me.

1   2   3   4   5

Consider: I'm often tempted to view God's greatest symbol of commitment to me as _____? What am I most tempted to write in the blank? Status? Bank account? Health of family? Success?

It's easy for me to believe that I'm God's workmanship.

1   2   3   4   5

Consider: What circumstances cause me to struggle most with believing that God has started a good work in me and is consistently investing in me?

Expectations
Overall, my expectations concerning God are being met.

        1   2   3   4   5

Consider: How has my church or faith tradition influenced my expectations concerning how I experience God?

I am comfortable with the level of intimacy I experience with *God the Father.*

        1   2   3   4   5

Consider: Who are the key individuals (pastors, teachers, friends) and experiences that have shaped my expectations in this? Was there a time when I felt I was more intimate with God the Father than I am now?

I am comfortable voicing unmet expectations to God.

        1   2   3   4   5

Consider: What expectations do I have concerning God that I have almost given up on (deeper intimacy, healing, a dramatic answer to prayer)?

STRENGTHENING YOUR CLIMATE WITH GOD
After taking a reading of your relational climate with God, the next step is to identify the areas that need attention and to set out to strengthen them. The Scriptures state that we should train ourselves to be godly (see 1 Timothy 4:7). Just as an athlete sets aside time in his or her schedule to train and makes sacrifices to achieve a goal, we need to make cultivating a healthy climate with God a priority. Do I take time to acknowledge God through regular times of prayer? Do I take time to reflect on and acknowledge that God is with me everywhere I go and scrutinizes the path before me (see Psalm 139:3)? Am I strengthening my commitment to him as I con-

template his unwavering commitment to me symbolized in Christ's death for me (see 1 John 2:2)? Does my level of trust in God reflect his holiness, faithfulness and trustworthiness? Are my expectations of God shaped by the Scriptures or by my personal experience of God or my particular faith tradition? With each component of our climate with God, we need to regularly pray as David did: "Search me, O God, and know my heart" (Psalm 139:23).

For our climate with God to flourish, we also have to address the difficult times mentioned by C. S. Lewis and King David when God seems distant or hidden. Every Christian I know can relate to times when the Christian life seems like one trial or difficulty after another. Why would God allow those he loves and watches over to experience such pain and hardship? Why would James write that when faced with a trial our response should be, "Consider it pure joy, my brothers, whenever you face trials of many kinds" (1:2).

First, trials have a unique way of surfacing what we think about God. A. W. Tozer wrote, "Only after an ordeal of painful self-probing are we likely to discover what we actually believe about God."[9] A necessary first step in building a healthy communication climate with God is first to assess accurately and honestly the condition of that climate. Trials bring us face to face not only with the God we publicly profess but also with a picture of God we harbor in our hearts. And the two may be dramatically different.

When I received the notices that both of my articles were rejected, it surfaced in me a lingering feeling I had that God was not committed to me. The rejection of those articles started a long discussion between me and the Lord about where I derived my status (in publications or in him) and whether I trusted him with my career aspirations. If it were not for that trial of rejection, my feelings toward God would not have surfaced.

Second, trials are God's means of maturing us. James writes that the goal of trials in the life of a believer is that she or he may "be mature and complete, not lacking anything" (1:4). Like any good parent, God wants to see us mature in faith; if he shielded us from every pain and struggle, we would never move past being sheltered spiritual adolescents. Remember my friend who lost his job? After two years of searching, he finally did land on his feet in a job that not only pays the bills but also is deeply rewarding. While he's not out of the financial woods yet, he looks back on those two years as time of deep wrestling with God when he learned much about himself and God's faithfulness. He now views his work, kids and wife with a whole new level of appreciation.

How much do you appreciate all the good gifts and provisions God has given you? Trials are often God's teachable moments where he takes the pain of a fallen world and uses it to mature us.

In a hurrysick world, times of Bible reading, meditation, prayer and attentiveness to our climate with God will not just happen. Training ourselves to be godly will, at times, seem like another thing to do on a long list of things that must get done. The temptation will be to put relationships that are tangible and visible ahead of a relationship with an invisible God.

To resist this pull toward putting the human over the divine, we need to remember C. S. Lewis's insight that opened this chapter and now closes this book: "Human beings can't make one another really happy for long. You cannot love a fellow creature fully till you love God." By being attentive to your communication climate with God, you'll also strengthen you're climate with the most important person in your life—your spouse. "When first things are put first," Lewis concludes, "second things are not suppressed but increased."[10]

Epilogue

*I*t was obvious the couple was not doing well.

I stood with them at the elevators, waiting to go up to our rooms during the first night of a weekend marriage conference. "How are you?" I asked. "Not too good," he said. She stood off to the side, waiting for the doors to open, tears running down her cheeks. "I don't think we are going to make it," he said. There was an awkward silence. The doors of the elevator opened, and a large group of people got on, separating me from this distraught couple.

That night in my hotel room, I asked God to revive this couple's troubled relationship during the course of one weekend. During the hectic schedule of the conference, I would occasionally pray for them when they came to mind.

Sunday morning, as I walked up to the podium to give the last talk, I saw a couple hugging each other, laughing. It was the same couple I had spoken with at the elevator. Both of them smiled as I walked up. Needless to say, I was curious what had turned around their climate in such a short time. In the few minutes we spoke, their words made a lasting impression.

"God's getting ahold of our hearts," was the first thing the husband said to me. The wife stood next to him, nodding. Over the course of the weekend, they had heard about God's love for each of them and how Christ had suffered to secure the forgiveness of their sins. God was now asking each of them to love and forgive each other as Christ had loved and forgiven them.

Listening to them talk made me think of an old pastor friend of mine who regularly says that marriage is the union of two good forgivers. As Peter Kreeft advised his grandchildren, any problem between people can be resolved if two things are present: forgiveness and determination. Our climate will change when the realization of God's forgiveness gets ahold of our hearts and we extend that forgiveness to our spouse.

This couple's marital climate also started to turn around because they remembered that weekend what so many of us easily forget: only God's love can truly satisfy us. The key to a satisfying marital climate is in fostering an intimate climate with God. Only by acknowledging and experiencing God's perfect love will we be free to acknowledge and embrace the imperfect love of our spouse.

"It's amazing what you forget about each other," the wife added as she took her husband's hand. It's true, isn't it? In our hurrysick world, we rush around doing the business of marriage and family, and we forget to notice the unique person we fell in love with in the first place. Like the hurried people in the middle of a D.C. metro rush hour who passed by without noticing a virtuoso playing a multimillion-dollar violin, we fail to stop and appreciate our spouse or acknowledge him or her. Yet for one weekend this couple did; they slowed down long enough to notice each other and to remember what had drawn them together. In one weekend they went from an I-You relationship (seeing each other in their prescribed roles) to an I-Thou relationship (cherishing what was unique about each other), and it revitalized the climate between them.

"We decided we're going to stick it out," the husband concluded. With so many couples today deciding to call it quits, it is essential in creating a healthy marital climate that the option of divorce is taken off the table. The foundation of commitment is the knowledge that you as a couple will have a future together. When I first met this couple, they didn't know if their marriage would "make it," and that insecurity was short-circuiting any attempt to improve the climate between them.

In her study of what holds couples together, interpersonal communication scholar Mary Lund discovered that more important than feelings of love, sexual attraction or passion was the intention to stay together.[1] Simply put, couples who committed to stay together *did*. During the course of the weekend, this couple's decision to "stick" to each other transformed their climate. As the book of Genesis states it, they had decided to cleave to each other (2:24).

All of us can be encouraged that this couple's climate could be turned around in a short time by shoring up commitment, acknowledging each other, rebuilding trust and allowing God to work. For sure, this couple is going to face storms in their marriage that will challenge the steps they took to improve their climate. These marital storms will be exacerbated when the environmental stresses of hurriedness, affluenza and a culture of divorce start to press in against them. Yet, by diligently checking the temperature of their marriage and making adjustments, they can maintain a healthy, intimate climate.

The same possibility of transformation is true for you. By applying the principles you've read about, you can restore and strengthen your marital climate in a fairly short time, with God's help. Your climate will be strengthened and transformed, not by having more conversations but by having conversations in an intimate and healthy climate. As the proverb reminds us, a word spoken at the right time is invaluable (25:11).

Resources

ABUSE

Steward, Donald. *Refuge: A Pathway Out of Domestic Violence and Abuse.* Birmingham, Ala.: New Hope, 2004.

Nason-Clark, Nancy, and Catherine Clark Kroeger. *No Place for Abuse: Biblical and Practical Resources to Counteract Domestic Violence.* Revised ed. Downers Grove, Ill.: InterVarsity Press, 2010.

COMMUNICATION SKILLS

Chapman, Gary. *The Five Love Languages: How to Express Heartfelt Commitment to Your Mate.* Chicago: Northfield, 1995.

Gushee, David P. *Getting Marriage Right: Realistic Counseling for Saving and Strengthening Relationships.* Grand Rapids: Baker, 2004.

Stone, Douglas, Bruce Patton and Shelia Heen. *Difficult Conversations: How to Discuss What Matters Most.* New York: Penguin, 1999.

CONFLICT RESOLUTION

Downs, Tim, and Joy. *Fight Fair: Winning at Conflict Without Losing at Love.* Chicago: Moody Publishers, 2004.

Markman, Howard, Scott Stanley and Susan Blumburg. *Fighting for Your Marriage*. San Francisco: Jossey-Bass, 2001.

DEVOTIONALS FOR COUPLES

Rainey, Dennis, and Barbara. *Moments with You: Daily Connections for Couples*. Ventura, Calif.: Regal, 2007.

Rice, Russ, Brad Silverman and Lisa Guest. *No Greater Love: A 90-Day Devotional to Strengthen Your Marriage*. Nashville: Thomas Nelson, 2010.

SPIRITUAL DISCIPLINES

Calhoun, Adele Ahlberg. *Spiritual Disciplines Handbook: Practices That Transforms Us*. Downers Grove, Ill.: InterVarsity Press, 2005.

Foster, Richard J., and Gayle D. Beebe. *Longing for God: Seven Paths of Christian Devotion*. Downers Grove, Ill.: InterVarsity Press, 2009.

THEOLOGY OF MARRIAGE

Allender, Dan, and Tremper Longman. *Intimate Allies: Rediscovering God's Design for Marriage and Becoming Soul Mates for Life*. Wheaton, Ill.: Tyndale House, 1995.

Thomas, Gary. *Sacred Marriage*. Grand Rapids: Zondervan, 2000.

Notes

INTRODUCTION

[1]Michele Weiner-Davis, *Divorce Busting: A Step-By-Step Approach to Making Your Marriage Loving Again* (New York: Simon and Schuster, 1992), p. 100.

CHAPTER 1: WHAT ARE COMMUNICATION CLIMATES?

[1]Ronald Adler, Lawrence Rosenfeld and Russell Proctor, *Interplay: The Process of Interpersonal Communication*, 10th ed. (New York: Oxford University Press, 2007), p. 302.

[2]For a slightly different take on climates, see the work of relational scholar Julia Wood. In her research on interpersonal climates, she reviewed seven hundred articles and books on personal relationships and concluded that satisfying climates are made up of investment, commitment, trust and comfort with relational dialectics (opposing tensions in every relationship, such as the competing desires for autonomy and connection). Julia T. Wood, *Interpersonal Communication: Everyday Encounters*, 6th ed. (Belmont, Calif.: Wadsworth, 2007). While Wood's work is extremely helpful, I see investment as being part of commitment and view dialectics as a series of expectations that ebb and flow in a relationship. My work in perspective-taking leads me to include acknowledgment as a core element of a marital climate.

[3]Martin Buber, *I and Thou* (New York: Scribner, 1970).

[4]Eugene Peterson, *Subversive Spirituality* (Grand Rapids: Eerdmans, 1997), p. 188.

[5]Ronald C. Arnett, "Existential Homelessness: A Contemporary Case for Dialogue," in *The Reach of Dialogue: Confirmation, Voice, and Community,* ed. Rob Anderson, Kenneth Cissna and Ronald Arnett (Cresskill, N.J.: Hampton Press, 1994), p. 238.

[6]See Jill Doner Kagle, "Are We Lying to Ourselves About Deception?" *Social Service Review,* June 1998, pp. 234-44; J. Veroff, "Marital Commitment in the Early Years of Marriage," in *Handbook of Interpersonal Commitment and Relationship Stability,* ed. W. Jones and J. Adams (New York: Plenum, 1999), pp. 149-62.

[7]Julie Wood, *Interpersonal Communication: Everyday Encounters,* 6th ed. (Belmont, Calif.: Wadsworth, 2007), p. 198.

[8]Mario Mikulincer, "Attachment Style and the Mental Representation of the Self," *Journal of Personality and Social Psychology* 69 (1995): 1203-15.

[9]Tim Stafford, *A Love Story* (Grand Rapids: Zondervan, 1977), p. 25.

CHAPTER 2: ENVIRONMENTAL PRESS

[1]Anne McGee-Cooper, *You Don't Have to Go Home from Work Exhausted* (New York: Bantam, 1992).

[2]Jeremy Rifkin, *Time Wars: The Primary Conflict in Human History* (New York: Henry Holt, 1987), p. 12.

[3]To read more about this event, go to <www.washingtonpost.com/wp-dyn/content/article/2007/04/04/AR2007040401721.html>.

[4]Some people mistakenly think that interpersonal communication is what takes place simply when two people communicate. Rather, interpersonal communication occurs when people take time to see each other as unique, cultivate personal knowledge of each other, and most importantly, carefully create histories of interaction based on shared meanings of words and events.

[5]Maxine Frith, "Couples Starved of Social Time, Study Finds," *The Independent,* UK edition, July 16, 2004, News, p. 2.

[6]Mari Clements and Howard Markman, "The Transition to Parenthood: Is Having Children Hazardous to Marriage?" in *A Lifetime of Relationships,* ed. Nelly Vanzetti and Steve Duck (Pacific Grove, Calif.: Brooks/Cole, 1996), pp. 290-310.

[7]Gerald Egan, "Listening as Empathic Support," in *Bridges Not Walls,* ed. John Stewart (New York: Random House, 1973), p. 210.

[8]John DeGraaf, David Wann and Thomas Naylor, *Affluenza: The All-Consuming Epidemic* (San Francisco: Berrett-Koehler, 2001), p. 38.

[9]Ibid., p. 2.

[10]Ibid., p. 4.

[11]Ibid., p. 36.

[12]Ibid., p. 48.

[13]To check out this study, go to the British Broadcasting Corporation (BBC) home page <www.bbc.co.uk/>, and search for "Rom-Coms 'Spoil Your Love Life,' " December 16, 2008 <http://news.bbc.co.uk/2/hi/uk_news/scotland/edinburgh_and_east/7784366.stm>.

[14]Ibid.

[15]Mary Anne McPherson Oliver, *Conjugal Spirituality: The Primacy of Mutual Love in Christian Tradition* (Kansas City: Sheed and Ward, 1994), p. 33.

[16]Kat Giantis, "When the Vow Breaks," MSN Entertainment <http://entertainment.msn.com/news/article.aspx?news=114177>

[17]See <www.weddingringcoffin.com>.

[18]Barna Group, "Born Again Adults Less Likely to Co-Habit, Just as Likely to Divorce" (August 6, 2001) <www.barna.org/barna-update/article/5-barna-update/56-born-again-adults-less-likely-to-co-habit-just-as-likely-to-divorce>.

CHAPTER 3: IMPROVING YOUR COMMUNICATION CLIMATE

[1]Clifford Coonan, "How Beijing Used Rockets to Keep Opening Ceremony Dry," *The Independent*, August 11, 2008 <www.independent.co.uk/sport/olympics/how-beijing-used-rockets-to-keep-opening-ceremony-dry-890294.html>.

[2]Michael Shaara, *For Love of the Game* (New York: Ballantine, 1991), p. 52.

[3]Douglas Stone, Bruce Patton and Shelia Heen, *Difficult Conversations: How to Discuss What Matters Most* (New York: Penguin, 1999), p. 106.

[4]John Gottman, *Why Marriages Succeed or Fail . . . and How You Can Make Yours Last* (New York: Fireside Books, 1994), p. 127.

[5]Erma Bombeck, "Marriage: The Last Chance to Grow Up," *(Fredericksburg, Va.) Free Lance-Star*, October 20, 1989, p. 27.

[6]Julia T. Wood, *Interpersonal Communication: Everyday Encounters*, 6th ed. (Belmont, Calif.: Wadsworth, 2007), p. 198.

[7]Gary Thomas, *Sacred Marriage* (Grand Rapids: Zondervan), p. 107.

[8]Wood, *Interpersonal Communication*, p. 198.

[9]Ibid.

[10]Tannen contrasts rapport-talk among women with "report-talk," where men use talk with other men to primarily get and hold attention, to negotiate and to impart information. Deborah Tannen, *You Just Don't Understand: Women and Men in Conversation* (New York: Ballantine, 1990).

[11]C. S. Lewis, *The Four Loves* (New York: Harcourt Brace Jovanovich, 1960), p. 96.

[12]Sue Johnson, *Hold Me Tight: Seven Conversations for a Lifetime* (New York: Little, Brown, 2008), p. 15.

CHAPTER 4: STRENGTHENING TRUST IN YOUR CLIMATE

[1]Quoted in Stephen M. R. Covey, *The Speed of Trust* (New York: Free Press, 2006), p. 8.

[2]The Ring of Gyges—mentioned by Plato in his famous work *The Republic*, bk. 2—renders a simple shepherd invisible, allowing him the freedom to ponder committing crimes without the worry of getting caught. If a person were free of all potential punishment, what moral road would it lead him or her down? This mythical ring would serve as the partial inspiration for J. R. R. Tolkien's all-consuming ring in *The Lord of the Rings*.

[3]Julia Wood, *Interpersonal Communication: Everyday Encounters*, 6th ed. (Belmont, Calif.: Wadsworth, 2007), p. 257.

[4]Laura Guerrero, "Attachment Theory: A Communication Perspective," in *Engaging Theories in Interpersonal Communication: Multiple Perspectives*, ed. Leslie Baxter and Dawn Braithwaite (Thousand Oaks, Calif.: Sage, 2008), pp. 295-307.

[5]Wood, *Interpersonal Communication,* p. 257.

[6]*Larry King Live,* "Elizabeth Edwards discusses tragedies, strengths" (May 12, 2009), posted on CNN Politics <www.cnn.com/2009/POLITICS/05/12/lkl.edwards.transcript/index.html>.

[7]Daniel Goleman, *Emotional Intelligence: Why It Can Matter More Than I.Q.,* 10th ed. (New York: Bantam, 2006).

CHAPTER 5: TALKING YOUR WAY INTO A SUPPORTIVE CLIMATE

[1]Jack R. Gibb, "Sensitivity Training as a Medium for Personal Growth and Improved Interpersonal Relationships," *Interpersonal Development* 1 (1970): 6-31.

[2]Julia Wood, *Interpersonal Communication: Everyday Encounters*, 6th ed. (Belmont, Calif.: Wadsworth, 2010), p. 208.

[3]Ibid., p. 211.

[4]Susan Scott, "Fierce Conversations," in *Bridges Not Walls*, 9th ed., ed. John Stewart (New York: McGraw-Hill, 2006), p. 49.

[5]William Wilmot, *Relational Communication* (New York: McGraw-Hill, 1995), p. 64.

[6]William Wilmot and Joyce Hocker, *Interpersonal Conflict,* 8th ed. (New

York: McGraw-Hill, 2010), p. 26.

[7]Ibid.

[8]Ed Wheat, *How to Save Your Marriage Alone* (Grand Rapids: Zondervan, 1983), p. 8.

[9]Walter A. Elwell, ed., *Evangelical Dictionary of Theology* (Grand Rapids: Baker, 1984), p. 657.

[10]Wheat, *How to Save*, p. 13.

CHAPTER 7: CALLING A TRUCE

[1]Stanley Weintraub, *Silent Night: The Story of The World War I Christmas Truce* (New York: Plume, 2001), p. 75.

[2]Allan Ross, *The Expositor's Bible Commentary: Proverbs*, vol. 5, ed. Frank E. Gaebelein (Grand Rapids: Zondervan, 1984), p. 185.

[3]John Gottman, *Why Marriages Succeed or Fail . . . And How You Can Make Yours Last* (New York: Fireside Books, 1994), p. 29

[4]Ibid., p. 57.

[5]Chris Brauns, *Unpacking Forgiveness: Biblical Answers for Complex Questions and Deep Wounds* (Wheaton, Ill.: Crossway Books, 2008), p. 100.

[6]This question is not only useful in determining what is important but also has strong gender implications. In his study of couples, John Gottman reported that men easily become flooded—emotionally and physically overwhelmed—when spouses confront them with lists of four or more things that they are not pleased with in the relationship or in them personally. His advice is that women limit their complaints to one or two so that men do not emotionally or physically shut down.

[7]Brauns, *Unpacking Forgiveness*, p. 57.

[8]The truce was eventually broken by nervous commanders who started to remove men from the front line and replace them with fresh troops unaware of the Christmas truce.

CHAPTER 8: CHANGING HOW WE VIEW CONFLICT

[1]This is not to suggest that all marital conflict is born out of sin. Some conflict is merely a difference of opinion, preference or even personality. However, I find that a majority of conflict stems from a deep-seated selfishness that seeks to put personal needs above those of a spouse or family, violating Paul's command to be others' centered (Philippians 2:3-4). This desire to put self first is fueled by sinful tendencies and is exacerbated by a culture that promotes and caters to selfish inclinations.

[2]Dan Allender and Tremper Longman III, *Intimate Allies* (Wheaton, Ill.:

Tyndale House, 1995), p. 287.

[3]Roxane S. Lulofs and Dudley D. Cain, *Conflict: From Theory to Action*, 2nd ed. (Needham Heights, Mass.: Allyn and Bacon, 2000), p. 11.

[4]Ronald B. Adler, Lawrence B. Rosenfeld and Russell F. Proctor, *Interplay: The Process of Interpersonal Communication*, 10th ed. (New York: Oxford University Press, 2007), p. 334

[5]The neglect response shouldn't be confused with the advice given during our discussion concerning a marital truce. In a marital truce, a spouse will temporarily choose not to address an issue while seeking to improve the overall climate, making communication about marital issues more effective.

[6]Kathryn D. Rettig and Margaret M. Bubolz, "Interpersonal Resource Exchanges as Indicators of Quality of Marriage," *Journal of Marriage and the Family* 45 (1983): 497-509.

[7]Adler et al., *Interplay*, p. 335.

[8]John Gottman, *Why Marriages Succeed or Fail . . . and How You Can Make Yours Last* (New York: Fireside Books, 1994), p. 24.

[9]Gary Thomas, quoting biblical scholar C. K. Barrett, in *Sacred Marriage* (Grand Rapids: Zondervan, 2000), p. 34.

[10]Ibid.

[11]Belinda Luscombe "Al and Tipper Gore Separate: Why Some Long Term Marriages End," *Time,* June 2, 2010 <http://news.yahoo.com/s/time/20100602/us_time/08599199333800>.

[12]Lewis writes, "There are two equal and opposite errors into which our race can fall about the devils. One is to disbelieve in their existence. The other is to believe, and to feel an excessive and unhealthy interest in them. They themselves are equally pleased by both errors and hail a materialist or a magician with the same delight." *The Screwtape Letters* (New York: Penguin, 1988), p. xix.

Chapter 9: Seven Principles for Making Disagreement Productive

[1]John Gottman, *The Seven Principles for Making Marriage Work* (New York: Crown Publishers, 1999), p. 130.

[2]Ibid., p. 131.

[3]Sally Planalp, *Communication and Emotion* (Thousand Oaks, Calif.: Sage, 1999).

[4]See Mark H. Davis, *Empathy: A Social Psychological Approach* (Boulder, Colo.: Westview Press, 1996); Elaine Hatfield, John T. Cacioppo and Rich-

ard L. Rapson, *Emotional Contagion* (Cambridge: Cambridge University Press, 1994).

[5]J. C. McCroskey and L. R. Wheeles, *Introduction to Human Communication* (Boston: Allyn and Bacon, 1976), p. 5.

[6]John Gottman, "The Roles of Conflict Engagement, Escalation or Avoidance in Marital Interaction: A Longitudinal View of Five Types of Couples," *Journal of Consulting and Clinical Psychology* 61 (1993): 6-15; N. Jacobson and John Gottman, *Why Men Batter Women* (New York: Simon and Schuster, 1998).

[7]Douglas Stone, Bruce Patton and Shelia Heen, *Difficult Conversations: How to Discuss What Matters Most* (New York: Penguin, 1999), p. 148.

[8]Ibid., p. 150.

[9]C. S. Lewis, *Mere Christianity* (New York: Macmillan, 1960), p. 89.

CHAPTER 10: THE NECESSITY OF FORGIVENESS

[1]Peter Kreeft, *Before I Go: Letters to Our Children About What Really Matters* (Lanham, Md.: Sheed and Ward, 2007), p. 26.

[2]Kelley noted that three ways couples, families or friends handle forgiveness are (1) direct forgiveness: forgivers tell offenders they are forgiven; (2) indirect forgiveness: individuals do not tell offenders they are forgiven, rather forgiveness is just understood and communicated indirectly through humor, hugs or acting normal; (3) forgive with conditions: transgressors are told they are forgiven with clear conditions (stay off the drugs or don't ever see forgiver again). Douglas Kelley, "The Communication of Forgiveness," *Communication Studies* 49 (1998): 255-71.

[3]Lewis Smedes, *The Art of Forgiving: When You Need to Forgive and Don't Know How* (Nashville: Moorings, 1996), p. 6.

[4]Quoted in John Stott, *The Cross of Christ* (Downers Grove, Ill.: InterVarsity Press, 1986), p. 1.

[5]Ibid., p. 24.

[6]Dallas Willard, *The Spirit of the Disciplines: Understanding How God Changes Lives* (San Francisco: Harper and Row, 1988), p. ix.

[7]Malcolm Gladwell makes a similar point in observing that people become experts in their fields only after doing something—painting, speaking, teaching, writing, playing tennis—for ten thousand hours. It is the years of cultivation, practice and preparation of a skill that allows them to perform in the moment. "No one has yet found a case in which true world-class expertise was accomplished in less time. It seems that it takes the brain this long to assimilate all that it needs to know to achieve true mas-

tery." Malcom Gladwell, *Outliers: The Story of Success* (New York: Little, Brown, 2008), p. 40.

[8]Smedes, *Art of Forgiving*, p. 39.

[9]Thanks to my colleague Todd Lewis for his thoughts on King David and our need to express emotions toward God.

[10]J. B. Phillips, *God Our Contemporary* (New York: Macmillan, 1960), p. 89.

[11]For a deeper study of why God allows bad things to happen, not only in our marriage but in the world, see J. P. Moreland and Tim Muehlhoff, *The God Conversation: Using Illustrations and Stories to Illustrate Your Faith* (Downers Grove, Ill.: InterVarsity Press, 2007), pp. 19-44.

[12]Smedes, *Art of Forgiving*, p. 91.

[13]Darrell Laurant, "Holocaust survivor, forgiveness is freedom," *(Lynchburg, Va.) News and Advance*, April 1, 2008, 1A.

[14]Ibid.

CHAPTER 11: HURRICANE WARNINGS

[1]"Rihanna talks about abuse from Chris Brown" (November 5, 2009), posted on Celebrity Buzz <www.blogs.chron.com/celebritybuzz/2009/11/rihanna_talks_about_abuse_from.html>.

[2]Facts taken from Julia Wood, *Gendered Lives: Communication, Gender, and Culture*, 8th ed. (Boston: Wadsworth, 2009); Donald Stewart, *Refuge: A Pathway Out of Domestic Violence* (Birmingham, Ala.: New Hope Publishers, 2004); Glen H. Stamp and Teresa Chandler Sabourin, "Accounting for Violence: An Analysis of Male Spousal Abuse Narratives," *Journal of Applied Communication Research* 23 (1995): 284-307.

[3]While female abuse of a male intimate partner is a reality, statistics show that it is predominantly the male who is responsible for domestic violence. Reflecting this reality, this chapter assumes the woman is the one being abused.

[4]Patricia Evans, *The Verbally Abusive Relationship: How to Recognize It and How to Respond* (Holbrook, Mass.: Adams Media Corporation, 1996), p. 81.

[5]David A. Hubbard, *Proverbs* (Dallas: Word, 1989), p. 277.

[6]Evans, *Verbally Abusive Relationship*, p. 81.

[7]Donald Stewart, *Refuge: A Pathway Out of Domestic Violence and Abuse* (Birmingham, Ala.: New Hope Publishers, 2004), p. 38.

[8]Evans, *Verbally Abusive Relationship*, p. 90.

[9]Beverly Engel, "Confronting Emotional Abuse," in *Bridges Not Walls*, 9th ed., ed. John Stewart (New York: McGraw-Hill, 2006), p. 277.

[10]Stewart, *Refuge*, p. 23.

[11]While it's easy for a male author to advocate calling 911, abused women understand that making such a phone call is often emotionally and physically challenging and has lasting implications. While a brief chapter on abuse in a book on marital communication doesn't allow me to dive into all the complexities surrounding this issue, allow me to affirm the right every Christian woman has to call the police if her husband is abusing her. According to the Scriptures, God has instituted civil authorities to curb and restrain evil (Romans 13:1-4). If your husband is hurting you physically, you are in danger, and he needs to be stopped.

[12]The woman who allowed me to use her story only asked that I change her name to one meaning *truth*. The Latin origin of *Vera* means "truth and faith" and is well fitting of her faith and courage.

[13]Debi Pryde and Don Stewart, "Are You Abusive? Three Questions for Husbands," posted on FamilyLife <www.familylife.com/site/apps/nlnet/content3.aspx?c=dnJHKLNnFoG&b=3855925&ct=4638779>.

CHAPTER 12: OUR COMMUNICATION CLIMATE WITH GOD AND WHY IT MEANS EVERYTHING

[1]W. H. Lewis, ed., *Letters of C. S. Lewis* (New York: Harcourt, Brace and World, 1966), p. 248.

[2]Wayne Grudem, *Systematic Theology* (Grand Rapids: Zondervan, 1994), p. 195.

[3]Ibid.

[4]C. S. Lewis, *A Grief Observed* (New York: Bantam, 1976), p. 4.

[5]Philip Yancey, *Disappointment with God: Three Questions No One Asks Aloud* (Grand Rapids: Zondervan, 1988), p. 22.

[6]Peter Kreeft, *Before I Go: Letters to Our Children About What Really Matters* (New York: Sheed and Ward, 2007), p. 34.

[7]John H. Coe, "Musings on the Dark Night of the Soul: Insights from St. John of the Cross on a Developmental Spirituality," *Journal of Psychology and Theology* 28, no. 4 (2000): 300. C. S. Lewis makes a similar point in the *Screwtape Letters* when he has a senior devil, Screwtape, make the following observation about God's interaction with his followers: "Sooner or later He withdraws, if not in fact, at least from their conscious experience, all those supports and incentives. He leaves the creature to stand up on its own legs—to carry out from the will alone duties which have lost all relish. . . . Hence the prayers offered in the state of dryness are those which please Him best" (C. S. Lewis, *The Screwtape Letters* [New York: Mentor Book, 1988], pp. 31-32).

[8]Tim Stafford, *Knowing the Face of God: The Search for a Personal Relationship with God* (Grand Rapids: Zondervan, 1986), p. 49.

[9]A. W. Tozer, *Knowledge of the Holy: The Attributes of God: Their Meaning in the Christian Life* (New York: Harper, 1961), p. 10.

[10]Lewis, *Letters of C. S. Lewis*, p. 248.

EPILOGUE

[1]Mary Lund, "The Development of Investment and Commitment Scales for Predicting Continuity of Personal Relationships," *Journal of Social and Personal Relationships* 2 (1985): 3-23.

Name and Subject Index